Allan Ramsey

The Tea-Table Miscellany

A Collection of Choice Songs, Scots and English Vol. 1

Allan Ramsey

The Tea-Table Miscellany
A Collection of Choice Songs, Scots and English Vol. 1

ISBN/EAN: 9783744774765

Printed in Europe, USA, Canada, Australia, Japan

Cover: Foto ©Thomas Meinert / pixelio.de

More available books at **www.hansebooks.com**

The Tea-Table Miscellany

VOLUME FIRST

The Tea-Table Miscellany

A COLLECTION

OF

hoice ongs

SCOTS & ENGLISH

By ALLAN RAMSAY

Reprinted from the Fourteenth Edition

IN TWO VOLUMES
VOLUME FIRST

Glasgow
JOHN CRUM, ST. VINCENT STREET
1871

Printed by R. CLARK, *Edinburgh.*

DEDICATION.

To ilka lovely BRITISH *laſs,*
  Frae Ladies Charlotte, Anne, *and* Jean.
Down to ilk bonny ſinging Beſs,
  Wha dances barefoot on the green.

DEAR LASSES,

YOUR moſt humble ſlave,
  Wha ne'er to ſerve you ſhall decline,
Kneeling, wad your acceptance crave,
  When he preſents this ſma' propine.

Then take it kindly to your care,
  Revive it with your tunefu' notes :
Its beauties will look ſweet and fair,
  Ariſing ſaftly through your throats.

The wanton wee thing will rejoice,
  When tented by a ſparkling eye,
The ſpinet tinkling with her voice,
  It lying on her lovely knee.

While kettles dringe on ingles dour,
   Or clashes stay the lazy lass;
Thir sangs may ward you frae the sour,
   And gaily vacant minutes pass.

E'en while the tea's fill'd reeking round,
   Rather than plot a tender tongue,
Treat a' the circling lugs wi' sound,
   Syne safely sip when ye have sung.

May happiness had up your hearts,
   And warm you lang with loving fires:
May pow'rs propitious play their parts,
   In matching you to your desires.

A. RAMSAY.

EDINBURGH, Jan. 1,
   1724.

PREFACE.

ALTHOUGH it be acknowledged that our Scots tunes have not lengthened variety of mufic, yet they have an agreeable gaiety and natural fweetnefs, that make them acceptable wherever they are known, not only among ourfelves, but in other countries. They are, for the moft part, fo chearful, that, on hearing them well played, or fung, we find a difficulty to keep ourfelves from dancing. What further adds to the efteem we have for them, is their antiquity, and their being univerfally known. Mankind's love for novelty would appear to contradict this reafon; but will not, when we confider, that for one that can tolerably entertain with vocal or inftrumental mufic, there are fifty that content themfelves with the pleafure of hearing, and finging without the trouble of being taught. Now, fuch are not judges of the fine flourifhes of new mufic imported from *Italy* and elfewhere, yet will liften with pleafure to tunes that they know, and can jŏin with in the chorus. Say that our way is only an harmonious fpeaking of merry, witty, or foft thoughts, after the poet has dreffed them in four or five ftanzas; yet undoubtedly thefe muft relifh beft with people who have not beftowed much of their time in acquiring a tafte for that downright perfect mufic, which requires none, or very little of the poet's affiftance.

My being well affured how acceptable new words to known tunes would prove, engaged me to the making verfes for above fixty of them, in this and the fecond volume: about thirty more were done by fome ingenious young gentlemen, who were fo well pleafed with my undertaking, that they generoufly lent me their affiftance; and to them the lovers of fenfe and mufic are obliged for fome of the beft fongs in the collection. The reft are fuch old verfes as have been done time out of mind, and only wanted to be cleared from the drofs of blundering tranfcribers and printers; fuch as, *The Gaberlunzieman, Muirland Willy,* &c., that claim their place in our collection for their merry images of the low character.

THIS fourteenth edition, in a few years, and the general demand for the book by perfons of all ranks, where-ever our language is underftood, is a fure evidence of its being acceptable. My worthy friend Dr. *Bannerman* tells me from *America*,

> *Nor only do your lays o'er* Britain *flow,*
> *Round all the globe your happy fonnets go;*
> *Here thy foft verfe, made to a* Scottifh *air,*
> *Are often fung by our* Virginian *fair.*
> Camilla's *warbling notes are heard no more,*
> *But yield to* Laft *time I came o'er the moor;*
> Hydafpes *and* Rinaldo *both give way*
> *To* Mary Scott, Tweedfide, *and* Mary Gray.

FROM this and the following volume, Mr. *Thomfon* (who is allowed by all to be a good teacher and finger of *Scots* fongs) culled his *Orpheus Caledonius,* the mufic for both the voice and flute, and the words of the fongs finely engraven in a folio book, for the ufe of perfons of the higheft quality in *Britain*, and dedicated to the late Queen. This, by the bye, I thought proper to intimate, and do myfelf that juftice which the publifher neglected; fince he ought to have acquainted his illuftrious lift of fubfcribers, that the moft of the fongs were mine, the mufic abftracted.

In my compofitions and collections, I have kept out all fmut and ribaldry, that the modeft voice and ear of the fair finger might meet with no affront; the chief bent of all my ftudies being to gain their good graces; and it fhall always be my care to ward off thofe frowns that would prove mortal to my mufe.

Now, little books, go your ways; be affured of favourable reception, where-ever the fun fhines on the free-born chearful *Briton;* fteal yourfelves into the ladies' bofoms. Happy volumes! you are to live too as long as the fong of *Homer* in *Greek* and *Englifh*, and mix your afhes only with the odes of *Horace*. Were it but my fate, when old and ruffled, like you to be again reprinted, what a curious figure would I appear on the utmoſt limits of time, after a thouſand editions? Happy volumes! you are ſecure; but I muſt yield, pleaſe the ladies, and take care of my fame.

In hopes of this, fearleſs of coming age,
    I'll ſmile thro' life; and when for rhyme renown'd,
I'll calmly quit the farce and giddy ſtage,
    And ſleep beneath a flow'ry turf full found.

INDEX

Beginning with the first line of every SONG.

―→•●•←―

The SONGS marked C, D, H, L, M, O, &c., are new words by different hands; X, the authors unknown; Z, old songs; Q, old songs with additions.

	PAGE
A COCK laird fou cadgie	204
A Southland Jenny that was right bonny .	192
Adieu, for a while, my native green plains .	138
Adieu, ye pleasant sports and plays . .	184
Ah, Chloe! thou treasure, thou joy, &c. . .	35
Ah! Chloris, cou'd I now but sit . . .	47
Ah! the shepherd's mournful fate . . .	91
Ah! why those tears in Nelly's eyes? . .	90
A lovely lass to a friar came	39
Altho' I be but a country-lass . . .	177
And I'll o'er the moor to Maggy . . .	66
An I'll awa to bonny Tweedside . . .	142
As early I walk'd, on the first of sweet May .	172
As from a rock past all relief . . .	53
As I came in by Teviot-side	195
As I sat at my spinning-wheel . . .	180
As I went forth to view the spring . .	101
As Sylvia in a forest lay	61
As walking forth to view the plain . .	68
At Polwart on the Green	67
At setting day and rising morn . . .	219
Auld Rob Morris that wins in yon glen . .	59

INDEX.

	PAGE
Balow, my boy, lie still and sleep	125
Beauty from fancy takes its arms	117
Beneath a beech's grateful shade	73
Beneath a green shade I fand a fair maid	78
Bessy's beauties shine sae bright	101
Blate Jonny faintly tald fair Jean his mind	25
Bless'd as th' immortal gods is he	113
Blyth Jocky young and gay	158
Bright Cynthia's power divinely great	36
Busk ye, busk ye, my bonny bride	139
Busk ye, busk ye, my bonny bonny bride	235
By a murmuring stream a fair shepherdess lay	17
By smooth winding Tay a swain was reclining	68
By the delicious warmness of thy mouth	77
Cauld be the rebels cast	212
Celestial muses, tune your lyres	29
Come, fill me a bumper, my jolly brave boys	49
Come, Florinda, lovely charmer	165
Come, here's to the nymph that I love	166
Come let's hae mair wine in	26
Confess thy love, fair blushing maid	123
Dear Roger, if your Jenny geck	210
Dumbarton's drums beat bonny—O	50
Duty and part of reason	217
Fair, sweet, and young, receive a prize	193
Farewell to Lochaber, and farewell my Jean	114
For the sake of somebody	191
Fy let us a' to the bridal	85
Gi'e me a lass with a lump of land	118
Gin ye meet a bonny lassie	76
Happy's the love which meets return	64
Harken, and I will tell you how	7

INDEX.

	PAGE
Have you any pots or pans	99
Hear me, ye nymphs, and ev'ry swain	2
Hid from himself, now by the dawn	214
Honest man, John Ochiltree	130
How blyth ilk morn was I to see	13
How happy is the rural clown	196
How shall I be sad when a husband I hae	211
How sweetly smells the simmer green!	1
I have a green purse, and a wee pickle gowd	176
I tofs and tumble through the night	146
I was anes a well tocher'd lafs	201
I will awa' wi' my love	65
I yield, dear lassie, ye have won	212
If love's a sweet passion, why does it torment?	129
In April, when primroses paint the sweet plain	43
In January last	133
In vain, fond youth; thy tears give o'er	37
In winter when the rain rain'd cauld	109
Is Hamilla then my own?	5
It was the charming month of May	124
Jocky fou, Jenny fain	187
Jocky met with Jenny fair	185
Jocky said to Jeany, Jeany, wilt thou do't	72
Lassie, lend me your braw hemp heckle	35
Late in an evening forth I went	115
Leave kindred and friends, sweet Betty	29
Let meaner beauties ufe their art	220
Let's be jovial, fill our glasses	6
Look where my dear Hamilla smiles	18
Love never more shall give me pain	56
Love's goddess in a myrtle grove	44
March, march	137
My dear and only love, I pray	106

	PAGE
My Jeany and I have toil'd	163
My Jocky blyth, for what thou'st done	60
My mither's ay glowran o'er me	63
My Patie is a lover gay	139
My Peggy is a young thing	209
My foger laddie is over the fea	205
My fweetest May, let love incline thee	72
Nanfy's to the Greenwood gane	20
Now all thy virgin-fweets are mine	181
Now from rusticity, and love	216
Now Phœbus advances on high	95
Now fpring begins her smiling round	152
Now the fun's gane out o' fight	75
Now wat ye wha I met yestreen	62
O Bell, thy looks have kill'd my heart	32
O Beffy Bell and Mary Gray	54
O come away, come away	159
O dear Peggy, love's beguiling	211
O had away, had away	159
O Jeany, Jeany, where has thou been?	202
O lovely maid, how dear's thy pow'r?	15
O Mary! thy graces and glances	92
O mither dear, I 'gin to fear	131
O Sandy, why leaves thou thy Nelly to mourn?	45
O steer her up, and had her gawn	98
O virgin kind! we canna tell	200
O waly, waly up the bank	179
O wha's that at my chamber door?	161
Of all the birds whofe tuneful throats	132
Of race divine thou needs must be	70
One day I heard Mary fay	135
Over the mountains	171
Pain'd with her flighting Jamie's love	52
Peggy, now the king's come	213

INDEX.   xvii

	PAGE
Return hameward, my heart, again	94
Rob's Jock came to woo our Jenny	174
Sandy in Edinburgh was born	151
Saw ye Jenny Nettles	186
Should auld acquaintance be forgot	51
Since all thy vows, falfe maid	140
Somnolente, quæfo, repente	136
Sound, found the mufic, found it	206
Speak on,—fpeak thus, and ftill my grief	217
Stately ftept he eaft the wa'	223
Subjected to the power of love	30
Sweet Sir, for your courtefie	57
Swift, Sandy, Young, and Gay	110
Teach me, Chloe, how to prove	17
Tell me, Hamilla, tell me why	31
Tell me, tell me, charming creature	37
The bonny grey-ey'd morning begins to peep	220
The carle he came o'er the croft	121
The collier has a daughter	89
The dorty will repent	210
The laird who in riches and honour	212
The lafs of Peaty's Mill	41
The laft time I came o'er the moor	40
The lawland lads think they are fine	87
The lawland maids gang trig and fine	157
The maltman comes on Munday	100
The meal was dear fhort fyne	26
The morn was fair, faft was the air	149
The night her filent fable wore	128
The pawky auld carle came o'er the lee	80
The fhepherd Adonis	119
The fun was funk beneath the hill	145
The widow can bake, and the widow can brew	156
The yellow-hair'd laddie fat down on yon brae	193
There was a wife won'd in a glen	103

INDEX.

	PAGE
This is not mine ain houfe	93
Tho' beauty like the rofe	3
Tho' for feven years and mair, honour, &c.	55
Thus let's ftudy night and day	194
Tibby has a ftore of charms	74
'Tis I have feven braw new gowns	22
'Tis not your beauty, nor your wit	162
'Twas at the fearful midnight hour	143
'Twas fummer, and the day was fair	38
Upon a fair morning, for foft recreation	107
Well, I agree, you're fure of me	216
Were I affur'd you'll conftant prove	215
What beauties does Flora difclofe?	4
What means this nicenefs now of late	59
What numbers fhall the mufe repeat?	88
When abfent from the nymph I love	120
When beauty blazes heavenly bright	167
When firft my dear laddie gade to the green hill	213
When flow'ry meadows deck the year	11
When hope was quite funk in defpair	218
When innocent paftime our pleafure did crown	33
When I think on my lad	96
When I've a faxpence under my thumb	161
When Phœbus bright the azure fkies	188
When fummer comes, the fwains on Tweed	150
When trees did bud, and fields were green	46
When we came to London town	32
When we meet again, Phely	10
Where wad bonny Annie lie?	83
While fops in faft Italian verfe	23
While our flocks are a-feeding	169
While fome for pleafure pawn their health	44
Why hangs that cloud upon thy brow?	12
Will ye go to the ew-bughts, Marion?	84
Willy, ne'er enquire what end	155

INDEX.

	PAGE
Willy was a wanton wag	197
With broken words, and downcaft eyes	79
With tuneful pipe and hearty glee	147
Ye blytheft lads and laffes gay	203
Ye gales that gently wave the fea	19
Ye gods! was Strephon's picture bleft	15
Ye powers! was Damon then fo bleft	10
Ye fhepherds and nymphs that adorn, &c.	48
Ye watchful guardians of the fair	42
Young Philander woo'd me lang	199

A COLLECTION

OF

CHOICE SONGS

Bonny Christy.

HOW sweetly smells the simmer green!
    Sweet taste the peach and cherry:
Painting and order please our een,
    And claret makes us merry:
But finest colours, fruits, and flowers,
    And wine, tho' I be thirsty,
Lose a' their charms, and weaker powers,
    Compar'd with those of Christy.

When wand'ring o'er the flow'ry park,
    No nat'ral beauty wanting,
How lightsome is't to hear the lark,
    And birds in concert chanting?
But if my Christy tunes her voice,
    I'm rapt in admiration;
My thoughts with ecstasies rejoice,
    And drap the haill creation.

Whene'er she smiles a kindly glance,
    I take the happy omen,
And aften mint to make advance,
    Hoping she'll prove a woman:

But, dubious of my ain defert,
　My fentiments I fmother;
With fecret fighs I vex my heart,
　For fear fhe love another.

Thus fang blate Edie by a burn,
　His Chrifty did o'er-hear him;
She doughtna let her lover mourn,
　But ere he wift drew near him.
She fpake her favour with a look,
　Which left nae room to doubt her:
He wifely this white minute took,
　And flang his arms about her.

My Chrifty! —— witnefs, bonny ftream,
　Sic joys frae tears arifing,
I wifh this may na be a dream;
　O love the maift furprifing!
Time was too precious now for tauk;
　This point of a' his wifhes,
He wadna with fet fpeeches bauk,
　But war'd it a' on kiffes.

The Bufh aboon TRAQUAIR.

HEAR me, ye nymphs, and ev'ry fwain,
　I'll tell how Peggy grieves me,
Tho' thus I languifh, thus complain,
　Alas! fhe ne'er believes me.
My vows and fighs, like filent air,
　Unheeded never move her;
At the bonny bufh aboon Traquair,
　'Twas there I firft did love her.

That day fhe fmil'd, and made me glad,
　No maid feem'd ever kinder;
I thought myfelf the luckieft lad,
　So fweetly there to find her.

I try'd to sooth my am'rous flame,
    In words that I thought tender;
If more there pass'd, I'm not to blame,
    I meant not to offend her.

Yet now she scornful flees the plain,
    The fields we then frequented;
If e'er we meet, she shows disdain,
    She looks as ne'er acquainted.
The bonny bush bloom'd fair in May,
    Its sweets I'll ay remember,
But now her frowns make it decay,
    It fades as in December.

Ye rural pow'rs, who hear my strains,
    Why thus should Peggy grieve me!
Oh! make her partner in my pains,
    Then let her smiles relieve me.
If not, my love will turn despair,
    My passion no more tender.
I'll leave the bush aboon Traquair,
    To lonely wilds I'll wander.   C.

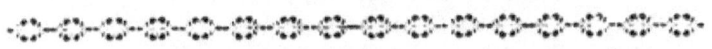

An ODE.

Tune—Polwart on the Green.

THO' beauty, like the rose
    That smiles on Polwart green,
In various colours shows,
    As 'tis by fancy seen:
Yet all its diff'rent glories ly,
    United in thy face,
And virtue, like the sun on high,
    Gives rays to ev'ry grace.

So charming is her air,
  So smooth, so calm her mind,
That to some angel's care
  Each motion seems assign'd:
But yet so chearful, sprightly, gay,
  The joyful moments fly,
As if for wings they stole the ray
  She darteth from her eye.

Kind am'rous Cupids, while
  With tuneful voice she sings,
Perfume her breath and smile,
  And wave their balmy wings:
But as the tender blushes rise,
  Soft innocence doth warm,
The soul in blisful ecstasies
  Dissolveth in the charm.

TWEED-SIDE.

WHAT beauties does Flora disclose?
  How sweet are her smiles upon Tweed?
Yet Mary's still sweeter than those;
  Both nature and fancy exceed.
Nor daisy, nor sweet-blushing rose,
  Not all the gay flow'rs of the field,
Not Tweed gliding gently through those,
  Such beauty and pleasure does yield.

The warblers are heard in the grove,
  The linnet, the lark, and the thrush,
The blackbird, and sweet-cooing dove,
  With music enchant ev'ry bush.
Come, let us go forth to the mead,
  Let us see how the primroses spring,
We'll lodge in some village on Tweed,
  And love while the feather'd folks sing.

How does my love pafs the long day?
  Does Mary not 'tend a few fheep?
Do they never careleflly ftray,
  While happily fhe lies afleep?
Tweed's murmurs fhould lull her to reft;
  Kind nature indulging my blifs,
To relieve the foft pains of my breaft,
  I'd fteal an ambrofial kifs.

'Tis fhe does the virgins excel,
  No beauty with her may compare;
Love's graces all round her do dwell,
  She's faireft where thoufands are fair.
Say, charmer, where do thy flocks ftray?
  Oh! tell me at noon where they feed;
Shall I feek them on fweet winding Tay,
  Or the pleafanter banks of the Tweed?

SONG.

Tune—*Wo's my heart that we fhould funder.*

IS Hamilla then my own?
  O! the dear, the charming treafure:
Fortune now in vain fhall frown;
  All my future life is pleafure.

See how rich with youthful grace,
  Beauty warms her ev'ry feature;
Smiling heav'n is in her face,
  All is gay, and all is nature.

See what mingling charms arife,
  Rofy fmiles, and kindling blufhes;
Love fits laughing in her eyes,
  And betrays her fecret wifhes.

Haſte then from the Idalian grove,
    Infant ſmiles, and ſports, and graces;
Spread the downy couch for love,
    And lull us in your ſweet embraces.

Softeſt raptures, pure from noiſe,
    This fair happy night ſurround us;
While a thouſand ſprightly joys
    Silent flutter all around us.

Thus unſour'd with care or ſtrife,
    Heav'n ſtill guard this deareſt bleſſing!
While we tread the path of life,
    Loving ſtill, and ſtill poſſeſſing.   S.

SONG.

LET'S be jovial, fill our glaſſes,
    Madneſs 'tis for us to think,
How the world is rul'd by aſſes,
    And the wiſe are ſway'd by chink.
      Fa, la, ra, &c.

Then never let vain cares oppreſs us,
    Riches are to them a ſnare,
We're ev'ry one as rich as Crœſus,
    While our bottle drowns our care.
      Fa, la, ra, &c.

Wine will make us red as roſes,
    And our ſorrows quite forget:
Come let us fuddle all our noſes,
    Drink ourſelves quite out of debt.
      Fa, la, ra, &c.

When grim death is looking for us,
    We are toping at our bowls,
Bacchus joining in the chorus:
    Death, be gone, here's none but fouls.
      Fa, la, ra, &c.

God-like Bacchus thus commanding,
　　Trembling death away ſhall fly,
Ever after underſtanding,
　　Drinking fouls can never die.
　　　　Fa, la, ra, &c.

Muirland Willie.

HARKEN, and I will tell you how
　　Young muirland Willie came to woo,
Though he could neither ſay nor do,
　　The truth I tell to you.
But ay he cries, Whate'er betide,
Maggy I'ſe ha'e to be my bride.
　　　　With a fal, dal, &c.

On his gray yade as he did ride,
With durk and piſtol by his ſide,
He prick'd her on wi' meikle pride,
　　Wi' meikle mirth and glee.
Out o'er yon moſs, out o'er yon muir,
Till he came to her daddy's door.
　　　　With a fal, dal, &c.

Goodman, quoth he, be ye within?
I'm come your doughter's love to win,
I care na for making meikle din;
　　What anſwer gi'e ye me?
Now, wooer, quoth he, wou'd ye light down,
I'll gi'e ye my doughter's love to win.
　　　　With a fal, dal, &c.

Now, wooer, ſin ye are lighted down,
Where do ye win, or in what town?
I think my doughter winna gloom
　　On ſic a lad as ye.

The wooer he stept up the house,
And wow but he was wond'rous crouse.
    With a fal, dal, &c.

I have three owsen in a plough,
Twa good ga'en yads, and gear enough;
The place they ca' it Cadeneugh:
   I scorn to tell a lie.
Besides, I ha'e frae the great laird,
A peat-pat, and a lang kail-yard.
    With a fal, dal, &c.

The maid pat on her kirtle brown,
She was the brawest in a' the town;
I wat on him she did na gloom,
   But blinkit bonnilie.
The lover he stended up in haste,
And gript her hard about the waste.
    With a fal, dal, &c.

To win your love, maid, I'm come here;
I'm young, and ha'e enough o' gear;
And for mysell you need na fear,
   Troth try me whan ye like.
He took aff his bonnet, and spat in his chow,
He dighted his gab, and he pri'd her mou'.
    With a fal, dal, &c.

The maiden blushed, and bing'd fu' la',
She had na will to say him na,
But to her daddy she left it a',
   As they twa cou'd agree.
The lover he gae her the tither kiss,
Syne ran to her daddy, and tell'd him this.
    With a fal, dal, &c.

Your doughter wad na say me na,
But to yoursell she has left it a',
As we could 'gree between us twa;
   Say, what'll ye gi'e me wi' her?

Now, wooer, quo' he, I ha'e nae meikle,
But fic's I ha'e ye's get a pickle.
  With a fal, dal, &c.

A kilnfu' of corn I'll gi'e to thee,
Three foums of fheep, twa good milk ky,
Ye's ha'e the wadding dinner free;
  Troth I dow do na mair.
Content, quo' he, a bargain be't;
I'm far frae hame, make hafte let's do't.
  With a fal, dal, &c.

The bridal-day it came to pafs,
With mony a blythfome lad and lafs;
But ficken a day there never was,
  Sic mirth was never feen.
This winfome couple ftraked hands,
Mefs John ty'd up the marriage bands.
  With a fal, dal, &c.

And our bride's maidens were na few,
Wi' tap-knots, lug-knots, a' in blew,
Frae tap to tae they were braw new,
  And blinkit bonnilie.
Their toys and mutches were fae clean,
They glanced in our ladfes' een.
  With a fal, dal, &c.

Sic hirdum, dirdum, and fic din,
Wi' he o'er her, and fhe o'er him;
The minftrels they did never blin,
  Wi' meikle mirth and glee.
And ay they bobit, and ay they beckt,
And ay their wames together met.
  With a fal, dal, &c.   Z.

The Promis'd Joy.

Tune—Carl an the King come.

WHEN we meet again, Phely,
 When we meet again, Phely,
Raptures will reward our pain,
And lofs refult in gain, Phely.

 Long the fport of fortune driv'n,
 To defpair our thoughts were giv'n,
 Our odds will all be ev'n, Phely.
  When we meet again, Phely, &c.

 Now in dreary diftant groves,
 Though we moan like turtle-doves,
 Suft'ring beft our virtue proves,
 And will enhance our loves, Phely.
  When we meet again, Phely, &c.

 Joy will come in a furprife,
 Till its happy hour arife;
 Temper well your love-fick fighs,
 For hope becomes the wife, Phely.
  When we meet again, Phely,
  When we meet again, Phely,
  Raptures will reward our pain,
  And lofs refult in gain, Phely.

To Delia, on her drawing him to her Valentine.

Tune—Black-ey'd Sufan.

YE powers! was Damon then fo bleft,
 To fall to charming Delia's fhare;
Delia, the beauteous maid, poffeft
 Of all that's foft, and all that's fair?

Here cease thy bounty, O indulgent heav'n!
I ask no more, for all my wish is giv'n.

I came, and Delia smiling show'd,
　　She smil'd, and show'd the happy name;
With rising joy my heart o'erflow'd,
　　I felt, and blest the new-born flame.
May softest pleasures careless round her move,
May all her nights be joy, and days be love.

She drew the treasure from her breast,
　　That breast where love and graces play,
O name beyond expression blest!
　　Thus lodg'd with all that's fair and gay.
To be so lodg'd! the thought is ecstasy,
Who would not wish in paradise to ly?　　R.

The Faithful Shepherd.

Tune—*Auld lang syne.*

WHEN flow'ry meadows deck the year,
　　And sporting lambkins play,
When spangl'd fields renew'd appear,
　　And music wak'd the day;
Then did my Chloe leave her bow'r,
　　To hear my am'rous lay;
Warm'd by my love, she vow'd no pow'r
　　Shou'd lead her heart astray.

The warbling quires from ev'ry bough
　　Surround our couch in throngs,
And all their tuneful art bestow,
　　To give us change of songs:
Scenes of delight my soul possess'd,
　　I bless'd, then hugg'd my maid;
I robb'd the kisses from her breast,
　　Sweet as a noon-day's shade.

Joy tranſporting never fails
    To fly away as air,
Another ſwain with her prevails
    To be as falſe as fair.
What can my fatal paſſion cure?
    I'll never woo again;
All her diſdain I muſt endure,
    Adoring her in vain.

What pity 'tis to hear the boy
    Thus ſighing with his pain;
But time and ſcorn may give him joy,
    To hear her ſigh again.
Ah! fickle Chloe, be advis'd,
    Do not thyſelf beguile,
A faithful lover ſhould be priz'd,
    Then cure him with a ſmile.

To Mrs. S. H. on her taking ſomething ill I ſaid.

Tune—*Hallow ev'n.*

WHY hangs that cloud upon thy brow?
    That beauteous heav'n ere while ſerene?
Whence do theſe ſtorms and tempeſts flow,
    Or what this guſt of paſſion mean?
And muſt then mankind loſe that light,
    Which in thine eyes was wont to ſhine,
And ly obſcure in endleſs night,
    For each poor ſilly ſpeech of mine?

Dear child, how can I wrong thy name,
    Since 'tis acknowledg'd, at all hands,
That could ill tongues abuſe thy fame,
    Thy beauty can make large amends:

Or if I durst profanely try
  Thy beauty's pow'rful charms t' upbraid,
Thy virtue well might give the lie,
  Nor call thy beauty to its aid.

For Venus every heart t' ensnare,
  With all her charms has deck'd thy face,
And Pallas, with unusual care,
  Bids wisdom heighten every grace.
Who can the double pain endure;
  Or who must not resign the field
To thee, celestial maid, secure
  With Cupid's bow, and Pallas' shield?

If then to thee such power is given,
  Let not a wretch in torment live,
But smile, and learn to copy heaven,
  Since we must sin ere it forgive.
Yet pitying heaven not only does
  Forgive th' offender and th' offence,
But even itself appeas'd bestows,
  As the reward of penitence.   H.

The Broom of Cowdenknows.

HOW blyth ilk morn was I to see
    The swain come o'er the hill!
He skipt the burn and flew to me:
    I met him with good will.
    O the broom, the bonny bonny broom,
      The broom of Cowdenknows;
    I wish I were with my dear swain,
      With his pipe and my ewes.

I neither wanted ewe nor lamb,
    While his flock near me lay:
He gather'd in my sheep at night,
    And chear'd me a' the day.
    O the broom, &c.

He tun'd his pipe and reed fae fweet,
   The burds ftood lift'ning by :
E'en the dull cattle ftood and gaz'd,
   Charm'd with his melody.
      O the broom, &c.

While thus we fpent our time by turns,
   Betwixt our flocks and play;
I envy'd not the faireft dame,
   Tho' ne'er fo rich and gay.
      O the broom, &c.

Hard fate that I fhould banifh'd be,
   Gang heavily and mourn,
Becaufe I lov'd the kindeft fwain
   That ever yet was born.
      O the broom, &c.

He did oblige me every hour,
   Cou'd I but faithfu' be ?
He ftaw my heart : Cou'd I refufe
   Whate'er he afk'd of me ?
      O the broom, &c.

My doggie and my little kit
   That held my wee foup whey
My plaidy, broach, and crooked ftick,
   May now ly ufelefs by,
      O the broom, &c.

Adieu, ye Cowdenknows, adieu,
   Farewel a' pleafures there ;
Ye gods, reftore me to my fwain,
   Is a' I crave or care.
      O the broom, the bonny bonny broom,
         The broom of Cowdenknows ;
      I wifh I were with my dear fwain,
         With his pipe and my ewes.   S. R.

To Chloe.

Tune—I wish my love were in a Mire.

O LOVELY maid, how dear's thy pow'r?
    At once I love, at once adore:
With wonder are my thoughts poffeft,
While fofteft love infpires my breaft.
This tender look, thefe eyes of mine,
Confefs their am'rous mafter thine;
Thefe eyes with Strephon's paffion play,
Firft make me love, and then betray.

    Yes, charming victor, I am thine,
Poor as it is, this heart of mine
Was never in another's pow'r,
Was never pierc'd by love before.
In thee I've treafur'd up my joy,
Thou canft give blifs, or blifs deftroy:
And thus I've bound myfelf to love,
While blifs or mifery can move.

    O fhould I ne'er poffefs thy charms,
Ne'er meet my comfort in thy arms;
Were hopes of dear enjoyment gone,
Still would I love, love thee alone.
But, like fome difcontented fhade
That wanders where its body's laid,
Mournful I'd roam with hollow glare,
For ever exil'd from my fair.   L.

Upon hearing his picture was in Chloe's breaft.

Tune—The fourteen of October.

YE gods! was Strephon's picture bleft
    With the fair heaven of Chloe's breaft?

Move softer, thou fond flutt'ring heart,
Oh gently throb,—too fierce thou art.
Tell me, thou brightest of thy kind,
For Strephon was the bliss design'd?
For Strephon's sake, dear charming maid,
Didst thou prefer his wand'ring shade?

And thou, blest shade, that sweetly art
Lodged so near my Chloe's heart,
For me the tender hour improve,
And softly tell how dear I love.
Ungrateful thing! it scorns to hear
Its wretched master's ardent pray'r,
Ingrossing all that beauteous heav'n,
That Chloe, lavish maid, has giv'n.

I cannot blame thee: Were I lord
Of all the wealth those breasts afford,
I'd be a miser too, nor give
An alms to keep a god alive.
Oh smile not thus, my lovely fair,
On these cold looks, that lifeless are;
Prize him whose bosom glows with fire,
With eager love and soft desire.

'Tis true, thy charms, O pow'rful maid,
To life can bring the silent shade:
Thou canst surpass the painter's art,
And real warmth and flames impart.
But oh! it ne'er can love like me,
I've ever lov'd, and lov'd but thee:
Then, charmer, grant my fond request,
Say thou canst love, and make me bless'd.

Song for a Serenade.

Tune—*The broom of Cowdenknows.*

TEACH me, Chloe, how to prove
   My boasted flame sincere;
'Tis hard to tell how dear I love,
   And hard to hide my care.

Sleep in vain displays her charms,
   To bribe my soul to rest,
Vainly spreads her silken arms,
   And courts me to her breast.

Where can Strephon find repose,
   If Chloe is not there?
For ah! no peace his bosom knows,
   When absent from the fair.

What tho' Phœbus from on high
   With-holds his chearful ray,
Thine eyes can well his light supply,
   And give me more than day.   L.

Love is the cause of my mourning.

BY a murmuring stream a fair shepherdess lay,
   Be so kind, O ye nymphs, I oftimes heard her say,
Tell Strephon I die, if he passes this way,
   And that love is the cause of my mourning.
False shepherds, that tell me of beauty and charms,
You deceive me, for Strephon's cold heart never
   warms;
Yet bring me this Strephon, let me die in his arms,
   Oh Strephon! the cause of my mourning.

>   But firſt, ſaid ſhe, let me go
>   Down to the ſhades below,
>   Ere ye let Strephon know
>   That I have lov'd him ſo :
> Then on my pale cheek no bluſhes will ſhow
>   *That love was the cauſe of my mourning.*
>
> Her eyes were ſcarce cloſed when Strephon came by;
> He thought ſhe'd been ſleeping, and ſoftly drew nigh;
> But finding her breathleſs, Oh heavens! did he cry,
>   *Ah Chloris! the cauſe of my mourning.*
> Reſtore me my Chloris, ye nymphs uſe your art.
> They ſighing, reply'd, 'Twas yourſelf ſhot the dart,
> That wounded the tender young ſhepherdeſs' heart,
>   *And kill'd the poor Chloris with mourning.*
>   Ah then, is Chloris dead,
>   Wounded by me? he ſaid;
>   I'll follow thee, chaſte maid,
>   Down to the ſilent ſhade,
> Then on her cold ſnowy breaſt leaning his head,
>   *Expir'd the poor Strephon with mourning.*   X.

To Mrs. A. H. on ſeeing her at a concert.

Tune—*The bonnieſt laſs in a' the warld.*

> LOOK where my dear Hamilla ſmiles,
>   Hamilla! heav'nly charmer;
> See how, with all their arts and wiles,
>   The Loves and Graces arm her.
> A bluſh dwells glowing on her cheeks,
>   Fair feats of youthful pleaſures,
> There love in ſmiling language ſpeaks,
>   There ſpreads his roſy treaſures.

O faireſt maid, I own thy pow'r,
  I gaze, I ſigh, and languiſh,
Yet ever, ever will adore,
  And triumph in my anguiſh.
But eaſe, O charmer, eaſe my care,
  And let my torments move thee ;
As thou are faireſt of the fair,
  So I the deareſt love thee.   2. C.

The Bonny Scot.

Tune—The boat-man.

YE gales that gently wave the ſea,
  And pleaſe the canny boat-man,
Bear me frae hence, or bring to me
  My brave, my bonny Scot—man :
    In haly bands
    We join'd our hands,
  Yet may not this diſcover,
    While parents rate
    A large eſtate,
  Before a faithfu' lover.

But I loor chuſe in Highland glens
  To herd the kid and goat—man,
Ere I cou'd for ſic little ends
  Refuſe my bonny Scot—man.
    Wae worth the man
    Wha firſt began
  The baſe ungenerous faſhion,
    Frae greedy views
    Love's art to uſe,
  While ſtrangers to its paſſion.

Frae foreign fields, my lovely youth,
　　Haſte to thy longing laſſie,
Who pants to preſs thy ba'my mouth,
　　And in her boſom hawſe thee.
　　　　Love gi'es the word,
　　　　Then haſte on board,
　　Fair winds and tenty boat-man,
　　　　Waft o'er, waft o'er
　　　　Frae yonder ſhore,
　　My blyth, my bonny Scot—man.

Scornfu' Nansy.

To its own Tune.

NANSY's to the Greenwood gane,
　　To hear the gowdſpink chatt'ring,
And Willie he has followed her,
　　To gain her love by flatt'ring:
But a' that he cou'd ſay or do,
　　She geck'd and ſcorned at him;
And ay when he began to woo,
　　She bid him mind wha gat him.

What ails ye at my dad, quoth he,
　　My minny or my aunty?
With crowdy mowdy they fed me,
　　Lang-kail and ranty-tanty:
With bannocks of good barley-meal,
　　Of thae there was right plenty,
With chapped ſtocks fou butter'd well;
　　And was not that right dainty?

Although my father was nae laird,
　　'Tis daffin to be vaunty,
He keepit ay a good kail-yard,
　　A ha' houſe and a pantry:

A good blew bonnet on his head,
    An owrlay 'bout his cragy;
And ay until the day he dy'd,
    He rade on good fhanks naggy.

Now wae and wander on your fnout,
    Wad ye hae bonny Nanfy?
Wad ye compare yourfell to me,
    A docken till a tanfie?
I have a wooer of my ain,
    They ca' him fouple Sandy,
And well I wat his bonny mou'
    Is fweet like fugar-candy.

Wow, Nanfy, what needs a' this din?
    Do I not ken this Sandy?
I'm fure the chief of a' his kin
    Was Rob the beggar randy:
His minny Meg upo' her back
    Bare baith him and his billy;
Will ye compare a nafty pack
    To me your winfome Willy?

My gutcher left a good braid-fword,
    Though it be auld and rufty,
Yet ye may tak it on my word,
    It is baith ftout and trufty;
And if I can but get it drawn,
    Which will be right uneafy,
I fhall lay baith my lugs in pawn,
    That he fhall get a heezy.

Then Nanfy turn'd her round about,
    And faid, Did Sandy hear ye,
Ye wadna mifs to get a clout;
    I ken he difna fear ye:
Sae had your tongue and fay nae mair,
    Set fomewhere elfe your fancy;
For as lang's Sandy's to the fore,
    Ye never fhall get Nanfy.   Z.

Slighted Nansy.

Tune—The kirk wad let me be.

'Tis I have seven braw new gowns,
    And ither seven better to mak,
And yet for a' my new gowns,
    My wooer has turn'd his back.
Besides, I have seven milk-ky,
    And Sandy he has but three;
And yet for a' my good ky,
    The laddie winna ha'e me.

My daddy's a delver of dikes,
    My mither can card and spin,
And I am a fine fodgel lass,
    And the filler comes linkin in,
The filler comes linkin in,
    And it is fou fair to see,
And fifty times wow! O wow!
    What ails the lads at me?

When ever our Baty does bark,
    Then fast to the door I rin,
To see gin ony young spark
    Will light and venture but in:
But never a ane will come in,
    Tho' mony a ane gaes by,
Syne far ben the house I rin;
    And a weary wight am I.

When I was at my first pray'rs,
    I pray'd but anes i' the year,
I wish'd for a handsome young lad,
    And a lad with muckle gear.
When I was at my neist pray'rs,
    I pray'd but now and than,
I fash'd na my head about gear,
    If I got a handsome young man.

Now when I'm at my laſt pray'rs,
 I pray on baith night and day,
And O! if a beggar wad come,
 With that ſame beggar I'd gae.
And O! and what'll come o' me!
 And O! and what'll I do?
That ſic a braw laſſie as I
 Shou'd die for a wooer I trow.

Lucky Nansy.

Tune—*Dainty Davie.*

WHILE fops in ſaft Italian verſe,
 Ilk fair ane's een and breaſt rehearſe,
While ſangs abound and ſenſe is ſcarce,
 Theſe lines I have indited:
But neither darts nor arrows here,
Venus nor Cupid ſhall appear,
And yet with theſe fine ſounds I ſwear
 The maidens are delited.

 I was ay telling you,
 Lucky Nanſy, lucky Nanſy,
 Auld ſprings wad ding the new,
 But ye wad never trow me.

Nor ſnaw with crimſon will I mix,
To ſpread upon my laſſie's cheeks;
And ſyne th' unmeaning name prefix,
 Miranda, Chloe, or Phillis.
I'll fetch na ſimile frae Jove,
My height of ecſtaſy to prove,
Nor ſighing—thus—preſent my love
 With roſes eke and lilies.

 I was ay telling you, &c.

But stay,—I had amaist forgot
My mistress and my sang to boot,
And that's an unco' faut I wat;
   But Nansy, 'tis nae matter.
Ye see I clink my verse wi' rhyme,
And ken ye, that atones the crime;
Forby, how sweet my numbers chyme,
   And slide away like water.
     I was ay telling you, &c.

Now ken, my rev'rend sonsy fair,
Thy runkled cheeks and lyart hair,
Thy half-shut een and hodling air,
   Are a' my passion's fewel.
Nae skyring gowk, my dear, can see,
Or love, or grace, or heaven in thee;
Yet thou hast charms anew for me,
   Then smile, and be na cruel.

   Leez me on thy snawy pow,
   Lucky Nansy, lucky Nansy,
   Dryest wood will eithest low,
   And, Nansy, sae will ye now.

Troth I have sung the sang to you,
Which ne'er anither bard wad do;
Hear then my charitable vow,
   Dear venerable Nansy.
But if the warld my passion wrang,
And say ye only live in sang,
Ken I despise a sland'ring tongue,
   And sing to please my fancy.
     Leez me on thy, &c.   Q.

A Scots Cantata.

The tune after an Italian manner.

Compofed by Signor Lorenzo Bocchi.

Recitative.

BLATE Jonny faintly tald fair Jean his mind;
   Jeany took pleafure to deny him lang;
He thought her fcorn came frae her heart unkind,
Which gart him in defpair tune up this fang.

Air.

O bonny laffie, fince 'tis fae,
   That I'm defpis'd by thee,
I hate to live, but O I'm wae,
   And unco fweer to die.
Dear Jeany, think what dowy hours
   I thole by your difdain:
Ah! fhould a breaft fae faft as yours,
   Contain a heart of ftane?

Recitative.

Thefe tender notes did a' her pity move,
With melting heart fhe lift'ned to the boy;
O'ercome fhe fmil'd, and promis'd him her love:
He in return thus fang his rifing joy.

Air.

Hence frae my breaft, contentious care,
   Ye've tint the pow'r to pine;
My Jeany's good, my Jeany's fair,
   And a' her fweets are mine.
O fpread thine arms, and gi'e me fowth
   Of dear inchanting blifs,
A thoufand joys around thy mouth
   Gi'e heav'n with ilka kifs.

The Toast.

Tune—Saw ye my Peggy?

COME let's ha'e mair wine in,
   Bacchus hates repining,
Venus loves nae dwining,
   Let's be blyth and free.
Away with dull—Here t'ye, Sir;
Ye'er miſtreſs, Robie, gi'es her,
We'll drink her health wi' pleaſure,
   Wha's belov'd by thee.

   Then let Peggy warm ye,
That's a laſs can charm ye,
And to joys alarm ye,
   Sweet is ſhe to me.
Some angel ye wad ca' her,
And never wiſh ane brawer,
If ye bare-headed ſaw her
   Kiltet to the knee.

   Peggy a dainty laſs is,
Come let's join our glaſſes,
And refreſh our hauſes
   With a health to thee.
Let coofs their caſh be clinking,
Be ſtateſmen tint in thinking,
While we with love and drinking,
   Give our cares the lie.

Maggie's Tocher.

To its ain tune.

THE meal was dear ſhort ſyne,
   We buckl'd us a' the gither;
And Maggie was in her prime,
   When Willie made courtſhip till her:

Twa piſtals charg'd beguefs,
    To gie the courting ſhot;
And fyne came ben the lafs
    Wi' fwats drawn frae the but.
He firſt fpeer'd at the guidman,
    And fyne at Giles the mither,
An ye wad gi's a bit land,
    We'd buckle us e'en the gither.

My doughter ye ſhall ha'e,
    I'll gi'e you her by the hand;
But I'll part wi' my wife by my fae,
    Or I part wi' my land.
Your tocher it fall be good,
    There's nane fall ha'e its maik,
The lafs bound in her fnood,
    And Crummie wha kens her ſtake:
With an auld bedden o' claiths,
    Was left me by my mither,
They're jet black o'er wi' flaes,
    Ye may cuddle in them the gither.

Ye fpeak right well, guidman,
    But ye maun mend your hand,
And think o' modeſty,
    Gin ye'll not quat your land:
We are but young, ye ken,
    And now we're gawn the gither,
A houfe is butt and benn,
    And Crummie will want her fother.
The bairns are coming on,
    And they'll cry, O their mither!
We have nouther pat nor pan,
    But four bare legs the gither.

Your tocher's be good enough,
    For that ye need na fear,
Twa good ſtilts to the pleugh,
    And ye your fell maun ſteer:

Ye ſhall ha'e twa good pocks
   That anes were o' the tweel,
The t'ane to had the grots,
   The ither to had the meal:
With an auld kiſt made of wands,
   And that ſall be your coffer,
Wi' aiken woody bands,
   And that may had your tocher.

Conſider well, guidman,
   We ha'e but borrow'd gear,
The horſe that I ride on
   Is Sandy Wilſon's mare:
The ſaddle's nane o' my ain,
   An thae's but borrow'd boots;
And whan that I gae hame,
   I maun tak to my coots:
The cloak is Geordy Watt's,
   That gars me look ſae crouſe;
Come fill us a cogue of ſwats,
   We'll mak na mair toom ruſe.

I like you well, young lad,
   For telling me ſae plain,
I married when little I had
   O' gear that was my ain.
But ſin that things are ſae,
   The bride ſhe maun come furth,
Tho' a' the gear ſhe'll hae,
   It'll be but little worth.

A bargain it maun be,
   Fy, cry on Giles the mither:
Content am I, quo' ſhe,
   E'en gar the hiſſie come hither.
The bride ſhe gade till her bed,
   The bridegroom he came till her;
The fiddler crap in at the fit,
   An' they cuddl'd it a' the gither.   Z.

SONG.

Tune—Blink over the burn, sweet BETTY.

LEAVE kindred and friends, sweet Betty,
    Leave kindred and friends for me:
Assur'd thy servant is steady
    To love, to honour, and thee.
The gifts of nature and fortune
    May fly by chance as they came;
They're grounds the destinies sport on,
    But virtue is ever the same.

Altho' my fancy were roving,
    Thy charms so heavenly appear,
That other beauties disproving,
    I'd worship thine only, my dear.
And shou'd life's sorrows embitter
    The pleasure we promis'd our loves,
To share them together is fitter,
    Than moan asunder, like doves.

Oh! were I but once so blessed,
    To grasp my love in my arms!
By thee to be grasp'd! and kissed!
    And live on thy heaven of charms;
I'd laugh at fortune's caprices,
    Shou'd fortune capricious prove;
Tho' death shou'd tear me to pieces,
    I'd die a martyr to love.   M.

SONG.

Tune—The bonny grey-ey'd morning.

CELESTIAL muses, tune your lyres,
    Grace all my raptures with your lays,
Charming, inchanting Kate inspires,
    In lofty sounds her beauties praise:

How undesigning she displays
   Such scenes as ravish with delight;
Tho' brighter than meridian rays,
   They dazzle not, but please the sight.

Blind god, give this, this only dart,
   I neither will, nor can her harm;
I would but gently touch her heart,
   And try for once if that cou'd charm.
Go, Venus, use your fav'rite wile,
   As she is beauteous, make her kind,
Let all your graces round her smile,
   And sooth her till I comfort find.

When thus, by yielding, I'm o'erpaid,
   And all my anxious cares remov'd,
In moving notes I'll tell the maid,
   With what pure lasting flames I lov'd.
Then shall alternate life and death
   My ravish'd flutt'ring soul possess,
The softest tend'rest things I'll breathe
   Betwixt each am'rous fond caress.   O.

SONG.

Tune—*The broom of Cowdenknows.*

SUBJECTED to the power of love
   By Nell's resistless charms,
The fancy fix'd, no more can rove,
   Or fly soft love's alarms.

Gay Damon had the skill to shun
   All traps by Cupid laid,
Until his freedom was undone
   By Nell the conquering maid.

But who can stand the force of love,
  When she resolves to kill?
Her sparkling eyes love's arrows prove,
  And wound us with our will.

O happy Damon, happy fair,
  What Cupid has begun,
May faithful Hymen take a care
  To see it fairly done. G.

SONG.

Tune—*Logan water.*

Vitas hinnuleo me similis, Chloe.

TELL me, Hamilla, tell me why
  Thou dost from him that loves thee run?
Why from his soft embraces fly,
  And all his kind endearments shun?

So flies the fawn, with fear opprefs'd,
  Seeking its mother ev'ry where,
It starts at ev'ry empty blast,
  And trembles when no danger's near.

And yet I keep thee but in view,
  To gaze the glories of thy face,
Not with a hateful step pursue,
  As age to rifle every grace.

Cease, then, dear wildness, cease to toy,
  But haste all rivals to outshine,
And grown mature, and ripe for joy,
  Leave mamma's arms, and come to mine. W.

A South-Sea Sang.

Tune—*For our lang biding here.*

WHEN we came to London town,
    We dream'd of gowd in gowpens here,
And rantinly ran up and down,
    In rising stocks to buy a skair:
We daftly thought to row in rowth,
    But for our daffin paid right dear;
The lave will fare the war in trouth,
    For our lang biding here.

But when we find our purses toom,
    And dainty stocks began to fa',
We hang our lugs, and wi' a gloom
    Girn'd at stockjobbing ane and a'.
If ye gang near the South-Sea house,
    The whilly wha's will grip your gear,
Syne a' the lave will fare the war,
    For our lang biding here.

Hap me with thy Petticoat.

O BELL, thy looks have kill'd my heart,
    I pass the day in pain;
When night returns, I feel the smart,
    And wish for thee in vain.
I'm starving cold, while thou art warm:
    Have pity and incline,
And grant me for a hap that charm-
    ing petticoat of thine.

My ravish'd fancy in amaze
    Still wanders o'er thy charms,
Delusive dreams ten thousand ways
    Present thee to my arms.

But waking think what I endure,
  While cruel you decline
Those pleasures, which can only cure
  This panting breast of mine.

I faint, I fail, and wildly rove,
  Because you still deny
The just reward that's due to love,
  And let true passion die.
Oh! turn, and let compassion seize
  That lovely breast of thine;
Thy petticoat could give me ease,
  If thou and it were mine.

Sure heaven has fitted for delight
  That beauteous form of thine,
And thou'rt too good its law to slight,
  By hind'ring the design.
May all the pow'rs of love agree,
  At length to make thee mine,
Or loose my chains, and set me free
  From ev'ry charm of thine.

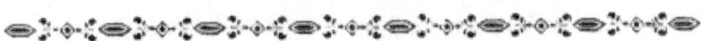

Love Inviting Reason.

A Song, Tune of—*Cha mi ma chattle, na duskar mi.*

WHEN innocent pastime our pleasure did crown,
  Upon a green meadow, or under a tree,
Ere Annie became a fine lady in town,
  How lovely, and loving, and bonny was she!
Rouse up thy reason, my beautifu' Annie,
  Let ne'er a new whim ding thy fancy a-jee;—
O! as thou art bonny, be faithfu' and canny,
  And favour thy Jamie, wha dotes upon thee.

Does the death of a lintwhite give Annie the fpleen?
　　Can tining of trifles be uneafy to thee?
Can lap-dogs and monkeys draw tears from thefe een,
　　That look with indiff'rence on poor dying me?
Roufe up thy reafon, my beautifu' Annie,
　　And dinna prefer a paroquet to me;
O! as thou art bonny, be prudent and canny,
' And think on thy Jamie wha dotes upon thee.

Ah! fhou'd a new manto or Flanders lace head,
　　Or yet a wee cottie, tho' never fae fine,
Gar thee grow forgetfu', and let his heart bleed,
　　That anes had fome hope of purchafing thine?
Roufe up thy reafon, my beautifu' Annie,
　　And dinna prefer ye'er fleegeries to me;
O! as thou art bonny, be folid and canny,
　　And tent a true lover that dotes upon thee.

Shall a Paris edition of new-fangle Sany,
　　Tho' gilt o'er wi' laces and fringes he be,
By adoring himfelf, be admir'd by fair Annie,
　　And aim at thefe benifons promis'd to me?
Roufe up thy reafon, my beautifu' Annie,
　　And never prefer a light dancer to me;
O! as thou art bonny, be conftant and canny,
　　Love only thy Jamie wha dotes upon thee.

O! think, my dear charmer, on ilka fweet hour,
　　That flade away faftly between thee and me,
Ere fquirrels, or beaus, or fopp'ry had power
　　To rival my love, and impofe upon thee.
Roufe up thy reafon, my beautifu' Annie,
　　And let thy defires be a' center'd in me;
O! as thou art bonny, be faithfu' and canny,
　　And love him wha's langing to center in thee.

The Bob of Dumblane.

LASSIE, lend me your braw hemp heckle,
  And I'll lend you my thripling kame;
For fainnefs, deary, I'll gar ye keckle,
  If ye'll go dance the *Bob of Dumblane*.
Hafte ye, gang to the ground of your trunkies,
  Bufk ye braw, and dinna think fhame;
Confider in time, if leading of monkies
  Be better than dancing the *Bob of Dumblane*.

Be frank, my laffie, left I grow fickle,
  And take my word and offer again.
Syne ye may chance to repent it mickle,
  Ye did na accept the *Bob of Dumblane*.
The dinner, the piper, and prieft shall be ready,
  And I'm grown dowy with lying my lane;
Away then, leave baith minny and daddy,
  And try with me the *Bob of Dumblane*.

SONG complaining of abfence.

Tune—*My apron, deary.*

AH Chloe! thou treafure, thou joy of my breaft,
  Since I parted from thee, I'm a ftranger to reft;
I fly to the grove, there to languifh and mourn,
There figh for my charmer, and long to return;
The fields all around me are fmiling and gay,
But they fmile all in vain—my Chloe's away;
The field and the grove can afford me no eafe,—
But bring me my Chloe, a defert will pleafe.

  No virgin I fee that my bofom alarms,
I'm cold to the faireft, tho' glowing with charms,
In vain they attack me, and fparkle the eye;
Thefe are not the looks of my Chloe, I cry.

These looks, where bright love, like the sun sits en-
    thron'd,
And smiling diffuses his influence round;
'Twas thus I first view'd thee, my charmer amaz'd,
Thus gaz'd thee with wonder, and lov'd while I gaz'd.

Then, then the dear fair one was still in my sight,
It was pleasure all day, it was rapture all night;
But now by hard fortune remov'd from my fair,
In secret I languish, a prey to despair;
But absence and torment abate not my flame,
My Chloe's still charming, my passion the same;
O! would she preserve me a place in her breast,
Then absence would please me, for I would be bless'd.

           R.

SONG.

Tune—*I fix'd my fancy on her.*

BRIGHT Cynthia's power divinely great,
 What heart is not obeying?
A thousand Cupids on her wait,
 And in her eyes are playing.
She seems the queen of love to reign;
 For she alone dispenses
Such sweets as best can entertain
 The gust of all the senses.

Her face a charming prospect brings,
 Her breath gives balmy blisses;
I hear an angel when she sings,
 And taste of heaven in kisses.
Four senses thus she feasts with joy,
 From nature's richest treasure:
Let me the other sense employ,
 And I shall die with pleasure.   X.

SONG.

Tune—I loo'd a bony lady.

TELL me, tell me, charming creature,
    Will you never eafe my pain?
Muſt I die for ev'ry feature?
    Muſt I always love in vain?
The defire of admiration
    Is the pleaſure you purſue;
Pray thee try a laſting paſſion,
    Such a love as mine for you.

Tears and fighing could not move you;
    For a lover ought to dare:
When I plainly told I lov'd you,
    Then you faid I went too far.
Are fuch giddy ways befeeming?
    Will my dear be fickle ſtill?
Conqueſt is the joy of women,
    Let their ſlaves be what they will.

Your neglect with torment fills me,
    And my deſp'rate thoughts increaſe;
Pray confider, if you kill me,
    You will have a lover leſs.
If your wand'ring heart is beating,
    For new lovers let it be:
But when you have done coquetting,
    Name a day, and fix on me.

The Reply.

IN vain, fond youth; thy tears give o'er;
    What more, alas! can Flavia do?
Thy truth I own, thy fate deplore:
    All are not happy that are true.

Suppress those sighs, and weep no more;
    Should heaven and earth with thee combine,
'Twere all in vain, since any power,
    To crown thy love, must alter mine.

But if revenge can ease thy pain,
    I'll sooth the ills I cannot cure;
Tell that I drag a hopeless chain,
    And all that I inflict endure.   X.

The Rose in Yarrow.

Tune—*Mary Scott.*

'TWAS summer, and the day was fair,
    Resolv'd a while to fly from care,
Beguiling thought, forgetting sorrow,
I wander'd o'er the braes of Yarrow;
Till then despising beauty's power,
I kept my heart, my own secure;
But Cupid's art did there deceive me,
And Mary's charms do now enslave me.

Will cruel love no bribe receive?
No ransom take for Mary's slave?
Her frowns of rest and hope deprive me;
Her lovely smiles like light revive me.
No bondage may with mine compare,
Since first I saw this charming fair:
This beauteous flower, this rose of Yarrow,
In nature's gardens has no marrow.

Had I of heaven but one request,
I'd ask to ly in Mary's breast;
There would I live or die with pleasure,
Nor spare this world one moment's leisure;

Despising kings, and all that's great,
I'd smile at courts, and courtier's fate;
My joy complete on such a marrow,
I'd dwell with her, and live on Yarrow.

But tho' such bliss I ne'er should gain,
Contented still I'll wear my chain,
In hopes my faithful heart may move her;
For leaving life I'll always love her.
What doubts distract a lover's mind?
That breast, all softness, must prove kind;
And she shall yet become my marrow,
The lovely beauteous rose of Yarrow.   C.

The Fair Penitent.

A Song.—*To its ain tune.*

A LOVELY lass to a friar came
    To confess in a morning early,
In what, my dear, art thou to blame?
    Come own it all sincerely.
I've done, Sir, what I dare not name,
    With a lad that loves me dearly.

The greatest fault in myself I know,
    Is what I now discover.
Then you to Rome for that must go,
    There discipline to suffer.
Lake-a-day, Sir! if it must be so,
    Pray with me send my lover.

No, no, my dear, you do but dream,
    We'll have no double dealing;
But if with me you'll repeat the same,
    I'll pardon your past failing.
I must own, Sir, tho' I blush for shame,
    That your penance is prevailing.   X.

The laſt time I came o'er the Moor.

THE laſt time I came o'er the moor,
    I left my love behind me.
Ye pow'rs! what pain do I endure,
    When ſoft ideas mind me?
Soon as the ruddy morn diſplay'd
    The beaming day enſuing,
I met betimes my lovely maid,
    In fit retreats for wooing.

Beneath the cooling ſhade we lay,
    Gazing and chaſtly ſporting;
We kifs'd and promis'd time away,
    Till night ſpread her black curtain.
I pitied all beneath the ſkies,
    Ev'n kings when ſhe was nigh me;
In raptures I beheld her eyes,
    Which could but ill deny me.

Shou'd I be call'd where cannons roar,
    Where mortal ſteel may wound me;
Or caſt upon ſome foreign ſhore,
    Where dangers may ſurround me:
Yet hopes again to ſee my love,
    To feaſt on glowing kiſſes,
Shall make my cares at diſtance move,
    In proſpect of ſuch bliſſes.

In all my ſoul there's not one place
    To let a rival enter:
Since ſhe excels in ev'ry grace,
    In her my love ſhall center.
Sooner the ſeas ſhall ceaſe to flow,
    Their waves the Alps ſhall cover,
On Greenland ice ſhall roſes grow,
    Before I ceaſe to love her.

The next time I go o'er the moor,
　　She fhall a lover find me;
And that my faith is firm and pure,
　　Tho' I left her behind me;
Then Hymen's facred bands fhall chain
　　My heart to her fair bofom,
There, while my being doth remain,
　　My love more frefh fhall bloffom.

The Lafs of Peaty's Mill.

THE lafs of Peaty's Mill,
　　So bonny, blyth, and gay,
In fpite of all my fkill,
　　Hath ftole my heart away.
When tedding of the hay,
　　Bare-headed on the green,
Love 'midft her locks did play,
　　And wanton'd in her een.

Her arms, white, round, and fmooth,
　　Breafts rifing in their dawn,
To age it would give youth,
　　To prefs 'em with his hand.
Through all my fpirits ran
　　An ecftafy of blifs,
When I fuch fweetnefs fand,
　　Wrapt in a balmy kifs.

Without the help of art,
　　Like flow'rs which grace the wild,
She did her fweets impart,
　　Whene'er fhe fpoke or fmil'd.
Her looks they were fo mild,
　　Free from affected pride,
She me to love beguil'd,
　　I wifh'd her for my bride.

O had I all that wealth
    Hopetoun's high mountains fill,
Insur'd long life and health,
    And pleasures at my will;
I'd promise and fulfil,
    That none but bonny she,
The lass of Peaty's Mill,
    Shou'd share the same wi' me.

Green Sleeves.

YE watchful guardians of the fair,
    Who skiff on wings of ambient air,
Of my dear Delia take a care,
    And represent her lover
With all the gaiety of youth,
With honour, justice, love, and truth;
Till I return, her passions sooth,
    For me in whispers move her.

Be careful no base sordid slave,
With foul sunk in a golden grave,
Who knows no virtue but to save,
    With glaring gold bewitch her.
Tell her, for me she was designed,
For me, who know how to be kind,
And have mair plenty in my mind,
    Than one who's ten times richer.

Let all the world turn upside down,
And fools run an eternal round,
In quest of what can ne'er be found,
    To please their vain ambition:
Let little minds great charms espy,
In shadows which at distance ly,
Whose hop'd-for pleasure, when come nigh,
    Prove nothing in fruition.

But caſt into a mold divine,
Fair Delia does with luſtre ſhine,
Her virtuous ſoul's an ample mine,
    Which yields a conſtant treaſure.
Let poets in ſublimeſt lays,
Employ their ſkill her fame to raiſe;
Let ſons of muſic paſs whole days,
    With well-tun'd reeds to pleaſe her.

The Yellow-hair'd Laddie.

IN April, when primroſes paint the ſweet plain,
  And ſummer approaching rejoiceth the ſwain;
The Yellow-hair'd Laddie would oftentimes go
To wilds and deep glens, where the hawthorn trees
    grow.

There, under the ſhade of an old ſacred thorn,
With freedom he ſung his loves ev'ning and morn:
He ſang with ſo ſaft and enchanting a ſound,
That ſylvans and fairies unſeen danc'd around.

The ſhepherd thus ſung, Tho' young Maya be fair,
Her beauty is daſh'd with a ſcornfu' proud air:
But Suſie was handſome, and ſweetly could ſing,
Her breath like the breezes perfum'd in the ſpring.

That Madie, in all the gay bloom of her youth,
Like the moon was inconſtant, and never ſpoke truth:
But Suſie was faithful, good-humour'd and free,
And fair as the goddeſs who ſprung from the ſea.

That mamma's fine daughter, with all her great
Was awkwardly airy, and frequently ſour: [dow'r,
Then, ſighing, he wiſhed, would parents agree,
The witty ſweet Suſie his miſtreſs might be.

Nanny—O.

WHILE fome for pleafure pawn their health,
    'Twixt Lais and the Bagnio,
I'll fave myfelf, and without ftealth,
    Kifs and carefs my Nanny—O.
She bids more fair t' engage a Jove
    Than Leda did or Danae—O.
Were I to paint the queen of love,
    None elfe fhould fit but Nanny—O.

How joyfully my fpirits rife,
    When dancing fhe moves finely—O;
I guefs what heaven is by her eyes,
    Which fparkle fo divinely—O.
Attend my vow, ye gods, while I
    Breathe in the blefs'd Britannia,
None's happinefs I fhall envy,
    As long's ye grant me Nanny—O.

Chorus.

My bonny, bonny Nanny—O,
My lovely, charming Nanny—O.
I care not tho' the world know
How dearly I love Nanny—O.

Bonny Jean.

LOVE'S goddefs in a myrtle grove,
    Said, Cupid, bend thy bow with fpeed,
Nor let the fhaft at random rove,
    For Jeany's haughty heart muft bleed.
The fmiling boy, with divine art,
    From Paphos fhot an arrow keen,
Which flew, unerring, to the heart,
    And kill'd the pride of bonny Jean.

No more the nymph, with haughty air,
　　Refuſes Willie's kind addreſs;
Her yielding bluſhes ſhow no care,
　　But too much fondneſs to ſuppreſs.
No more the youth is ſullen now,
　　But looks the gayeſt on the green,
While ev'ry day he ſpies ſome new
　　Surpriſing charms in bonny Jean.

A thouſand tranſports croud his breaſt,
　　He moves as light as fleeting wind,
His former ſorrows ſeem a jeſt,
　　Now when his Jeany is turn'd kind.
Riches he looks on with diſdain,
　　The glorious fields of war look mean;
The chearful hound and horn give pain,
　　If abſent from his bonny Jean.

The day he ſpends in am'rous gaze,
　　Which ev'n in ſummer ſhorten'd ſeems;
When funk in downs, with glad amaze,
　　He wonders at her in his dreams.
All charms diſcloſ'd, ſhe looks more bright
　　Than Troy's prize, the Spartan queen,
With breaking day, he lifts his fight,
　　And pants to be with bonny Jean.

Throw the Wood, Laddie.

O SANDY, why leaves thou thy Nelly to mourn?
　　Thy preſence could eaſe me,
　　When naething can pleaſe me;
Now dowie I ſigh on the bank of the burn,
Or throw the wood, laddie, until thou return.

Tho' woods now are bonny, and mornings are clear,
    While lav'rocks are finging,
    And primrofes fpringing;
Yet nane of them pleafes my eye or my ear,
When throw the wood, laddie, ye dinna appear.

That I am forfaken, fome fpare not to tell:
    I'm fafh'd wi' their fcorning,
    Baith ev'ning and morning;
Their jeering gaes aft to my heart wi' a knell,
When throw the wood, laddie, I wander myfell.

Then ftay, my dear Sandy, nae langer away,
    But quick as an arrow,
    Haft here to thy marrow,
Wha's living in languor till that happy day,
When throw the wood, laddie, we'll dance, fing, and
    play.

Down the Burn, Davie.

WHEN trees did bud, and fields were green,
    And broom bloom'd fair to fee;
When Mary was complete fifteen,
    And love laughed in her eye;
Blyth Davie's blinks her heart did move
    To fpeak her mind thus free,
Gang down the burn, Davie, love,
    And I fhall follow thee.

Now Davie did each lad furpafs,
    That dwelt on this burn-fide,
And Mary was the bonnieft lafs,
    Juft meet to be a bride;
Her cheeks were rofy, red, and white,
    Her e'en were bonny blue;
Her looks were like Aurora bright,
    Her lips like dropping dew.

As down the burn they took their way,
  What tender tales they faid!
His cheek to hers he aft did lay,
  And with her bofom play'd;
Till baith at length impatient grown,
  To be mair fully bleft,
In yonder vale they lean'd them down;
  Love only faw the reft.

What pafs'd, I guefs, was harmlefs play,
  And naething fure unmeet;
For, ganging hame, I heard them fay,
  They lik'd a wawk fae fweet;
And that they aften fhou'd return
  Sic pleafure to renew.
Quoth Mary, Love, I like the burn,
  And ay fhall follow you.   C.

SONG.

Tune—*Guilder Roy*.

AH! Chloris, cou'd I now but fit
    As unconcern'd, as when
Your infant beauty cou'd beget
    No happinefs nor pain.
When I this dawning did admire,
    And prais'd the coming day,
I little thought that rifing fire
    Wou'd take my reft away.

Your charms in harmlefs childhood lay,
    As metals in a mine.
Age from no face takes more away,
    Than youth conceal'd in thine:
But as your charms infenfibly
    To their perfection preft;
So love as unperceiv'd did fly,
    And center'd in my breaft.

My paſſion with your beauty grew,
　　While Cupid at my heart,
Still as his mother favour'd you,
　　Threw a new flaming dart:
Each gloried in their wanton part;
　　To make a lover, he
Employ'd the utmoſt of his art;—
　　To make a beauty, ſhe.

SONG.

Tune—*The Yellow-hair'd Laddie.*

YE ſhepherds and nymphs that adorn the gay plain,
　　Approach from your ſports, and attend to my
　　　　ſtrain;
Amongſt all your number a lover ſo true,
Was ne'er ſo undone, with ſuch bliſs in his view.

　　Was ever a nymph ſo hard-hearted as mine?
She knows me ſincere, and ſhe ſees how I pine;
She does not diſdain me, nor frown in her wrath,
But calmly and mildly reſigns me to death.

　　She calls me her friend, but her lover denies:
She ſmiles when I'm chearful, but hears not my ſighs;
A boſom ſo flinty, ſo gentle an air,
Inſpires me with hope, and yet bids me deſpair!

　　I fall at her feet, and implore her with tears:
Her anſwer confounds, while her manner endears;
When ſoftly ſhe tells me to hope no relief,
My trembling lips bleſs her in ſpite of my grief.

　　By night, while I ſlumber, ſtill haunted with care,
I ſtart up in anguiſh, and ſigh for the fair:
The fair ſleeps in peace, may ſhe ever do ſo!
And only when dreaming imagine my wo.

Then gaze at a distance, nor farther aspire;
Nor think she shou'd love, whom she cannot admire;
Hush all thy complaining, and dying her slave,
Commend her to heaven, and thyself to the grave.

SONG.

Tune—*When she came ben she bobbed.*

COME, fill me a bumper, my jolly brave boys,
Let's have no more female impert'nence and noise;
For I've try'd the endearments and pleasures of love,
And I find they're but nonsense and whimsies, by Jove.

When first of all Betty and I were acquaint,
I whin'd like a fool, and she sigh'd like a saint:
But I found her *religion*, her *face*, and her *love*,
Were *hypocrisy, paint,* and *self-interest,* by Jove.

Sweet Cecil came next with her languishing air,
Her *outside* was orderly, modest, and fair;
But her *soul* was *sophisticate*, so was her *love*,
For I found she was only a strumpet, by Jove.

Little double-gilt Jenny's gold charm'd me at last:
(You know *marriage* and *money together* does best.)
But the *baggage*, forgetting her *vows* and her *love*,
Gave her gold to a *sniv'ling dull coxcomb*, by Jove.

Come fill me a bumper then, jolly brave boys;
Here's a farewell to female impert'nence and noise:
I know few of the sex that are worthy my love;
And for *strumpets and jilts*, I abhor them, by Jove.
L.

Dumbarton's Drums.

Dumbarton's drums beat bonny—O,
  When they mind me of my dear Jonny—O.
    How happy am I,
    When my soldier is by,
While he kisses and blesses his Annie—O!
'Tis a soldier alone can delight me—O,
For his graceful looks do invite me—O:
    While guarded in his arms,
    I'll fear no war's alarms,
Neither danger nor death shall e'er fright me—O.

  My love is a handsome laddie—O,
Genteel, but ne'er foppish nor gaudy—O:
    Tho' commissions are dear,
    Yet I'll buy him one this year;
For he shall serve no longer a cadie—O.
A soldier has honour and bravery—O,
Unacquainted with rogues and their knavery—O;
    He minds no other thing
    But the ladies or the king;
For ev'ry other care is but slavery—O.

  Then I'll be the captain's lady—O;
Farewell all my friends and my daddy—O;
    I'll wait no more at home,
    But I'll follow with the drum,
And whene'er that beats, I'll be ready—O.
Dumbarton's drums sound bonny—O,
They are sprightly like my dear Jonny—O:
    How happy shall I be,
    When on my soldier's knee,
And he kisses and blesses his Annie—O!

Auld lang fyne.

SHOULD auld acquaintance be forgot,
    Tho' they return with fcars?
Thefe are the noble hero's lot,
    Obtain'd in glorious wars:
Welcome, my VARO, to my breaft,
    Thy arms about me twine,
And make me once again as bleft,
    As I was lang fyne.

Methinks around us on each bough,
    A thoufand cupids play,
Whilft thro' the groves I walk with you,
    Each object makes me gay:
Since your return the fun and moon
    With brighter beams do fhine;
Streams murmur foft notes while they run,
    As they did lang fyne.

Defpife the court and din of ftate;
    Let that to their fhare fall,
Who can efteem fuch flav'ry great,
    While bounded like a ball:
But funk in love, upon my arms
    Let your brave head recline;
We'll pleafe ourfelves with mutual charms,
    As we did lang fyne.

O'er moor and dale, with your gay friend,
    You may purfue the chace,
And, after a blyth bottle, end
    All cares in my embrace:
And in a vacant rainy day
    You fhall be wholly mine;
We'll make the hours run fmooth away,
    And laugh at lang fyne.

The hero, pleas'd with the sweet air,
　　And signs of gen'rous love,
Which had been utter'd by the fair,
　　Bow'd to the powers above:
Next day, with consent and glad haste,
　　Th' approach'd the sacred shrine;
Where the good priest the couple blest,
　　And put them out of pine.

The Lass of Livingston.

PAIN'D with her slighting Jamie's love,
　　Bell dropt a tear—Bell dropt a tear;
The gods descended from above,
Well pleas'd to hear—well pleas'd to hear.
They heard the praises of the youth
From her own tongue—from her own tongue,
Who now converted was to truth,
And thus she sung—and thus she sung.

　　Bless'd days when our ingenuous sex,
More frank and kind—more frank and kind,
Did not their lov'd adorers vex,
But spoke their mind—but spoke their mind.
Repenting now, she promis'd fair
Wou'd he return—wou'd he return,
She ne'er again wou'd give him care,
Or cause him mourn—or cause him mourn.

　　Why lov'd I thee, deserving swain,
Yet still thought shame—yet still thought shame,
When he my yielding heart did gain,
To own my flame—to own my flame?
Why took I pleasure to torment,
And seem too coy—and seem too coy?
Which makes me now, alas! lament
My slighted joy—my slighted joy.

Ye fair, while beauty's in its fpring,
Own your defire—own your defire,
While love's young power with his foft wing
Fans up the fire—fans up the fire.
O do not with a filly pride,
Or low defign—or low defign,
Refufe to be a happy bride,
But anfwer plain—but anfwer plain.

Thus the fair mourner wail'd her crime,
With flowing eyes—with flowing eyes.
Glad Jamie heard her all the time,
With fweet furprife—with fweet furprife.
Some god had led him to the grove;
His mind unchang'd—his mind unchang'd,
Flew to her arms, and cry'd, My love,
I am reveng'd—I am reveng'd!

PEGGY, I muft love thee.

AS from a rock paft all relief,
  The fhipwreck'd Colin fpying
His native foil, o'ercome with grief,
  Half funk in waves, and dying:
With the next morning-fun he fpies
A fhip, which gives unhop'd furprife;
New life fprings up, he lifts his eyes
  With joy, and waits her motion.

So when by her whom long I lov'd,
  I fcorn'd was, and deferted,
Low with defpair my fpirits mov'd,
  To be for ever parted:
Thus droop'd I, till diviner grace
I found in Peggy's mind and face;
Ingratitude appear'd then bafe,
  But virtue more engaging.

Then now ſince happily I've hit,
   I'll have no more delaying;
Let beauty yield to manly wit,
   We loſe ourſelves in ſtaying:
I'll haſte dull courtſhip to a cloſe,
Since marriage can my fears oppoſe:
Why ſhould we happy minutes loſe,
   Since, Peggy, I muſt love thee?

Men may be fooliſh, if they pleaſe,
   And deem't a lover's duty,
To ſigh, and ſacrifice their eaſe,
   Doting on a proud beauty:
Such was my caſe for many a year,
Still hope ſucceeding to my fear;
Falſe Betty's charms now diſappear,
   Since Peggy's far outſhine them.

Bessy Bell and Mary Gray.

O Beſſy Bell and Mary Gray,
   They are twa bonny laſſies,
They bigg'd a bow'r on yon burn-brae,
   And theek'd it o'er wi' raſhes.
Fair Beſſy Bell I loo'd yeſtreen,
   And thought I ne'er could alter;
But Mary Gray's twa pawky een,
   They gar my fancy falter.

Now Beſſy's hair's like a lint-tap;
   She ſmiles like a May morning,
When Phœbus ſtarts frae Thetis' lap,
   The hills with rays adorning:
White is her neck, ſaft is her hand,
   Her waiſt and feet's fu' genty;
With ilka grace ſhe can command;
   Her lips, O wow! they're dainty.

And Mary's locks are like a craw,
  Her een like diamonds glances;
She's ay fae clean, redd up, and braw,
  She kills whene'er fhe dances:
Blyth as a kid, with wit at will,
  She blooming, tight, and tall is;
And guides her airs fae gracefu' ftill,
  O Jove, fhe's like thy Pallas.

Dear Beffy Bell and Mary Gray,
  Ye unco fair opprefs us;
Our fancies jee between you twa,
  Ye are fic bonny laffies:
Wae's me! for baith I canna get,
  To ane by law we're ftented;
Then I'll draw cuts, and take my fate,
  And be with ane contented.

I'll never leave thee.

JONNY.

THO' for feven years and mair, honour fhou'd reave
      me,   [thee:
To fields where cannons rair, thou need na grieve
For deep in my fpirits thy fweets are indented;
And love fhall preferve ay what love has imprinted.
Leave thee, leave thee, I'll never leave thee,
Gang the warld as it will, deareft, believe me.

NELLY.

O Jonny, I'm jealous whene'er ye difcover
My fentiments yielding, ye'll turn a loofe rover;
And nought i' the warld wad vex my heart fairer,
If you prove unconftant, and fancy ane fairer.
Grieve me, grieve me, oh, it wad grieve me!
A' the lang night and day, if you deceive me.

Jonny.

My Nelly, let never fic fancies opprefs ye,
For while my blood's warm, I'll kindly carefs ye:
Your blooming faft beauties firft beeted love's fire,
Your virtue and wit make it ay flame the higher.
Leave thee, leave thee, I'll never leave thee,
Gang the warld as it will, deareft, believe me.

Nelly.

Then, Jonny, I frankly this minute allow ye
To think me your miftrefs, for love gars me trow ye:
And gin you prove faufe, to ye'rfell be it faid then,
Ye'll win but fma' honour to wrong a kind maiden.
Reave me, reave me, heav'ns! it wad reave me
Of my reft night and day, if ye deceive me.

Jonny.

Bid icefhogles hammer red gauds on the ftuddy,
And fair fimmer-mornings nae mair appear ruddy,
Bid Britons think ae gate, and when they obey ye,
But never till that time, believe I'll betray ye.
Leave thee, leave thee, I'll never leave thee;
The ftarns fhall gang witherfhins ere I deceive thee.

My Deary, if you die.

LOVE never more fhall give me pain,
   My fancy's fix'd on thee;
Nor ever maid my heart fhall gain,
   My Peggy, if thou die.
Thy beauties did fuch pleafure give,
   Thy love's fo true to me:
Without thee I fhall never live,
   My deary, if thou die.

If fate shall tear thee from my breast,
  How shall I lonely stray?
In dreary dreams the night I'll waste,
  In sighs the silent day.
I ne'er can so much virtue find,
  Nor such perfection see:
Then I'll renounce all womankind,
  My Peggy, after thee.

No new-blown beauty fires my heart
  With Cupid's raving rage,
But thine which can such sweets impart,
  Must all the world engage.
'Twas this that like the morning sun
  Gave joy and life to me;
And when its destin'd day is done,
  With Peggy let me die.

Ye pow'rs that smile on virtuous love,
  And in such pleasure share;
You who its faithful flames approve,
  With pity view the fair.
Restore my Peggy's wonted charms,
  Those charms so dear to me;
Oh! never rob them from those arms:
  I'm lost if Peggy die.

My Jo Janet.

SWEET Sir, for your courtesie,
  When ye come by the Bass then,
For the love you bear to me,
  Buy me a keeking-glass then.
Keek into the draw-well,
  Janet, Janet;
And there ye'll see ye'r bonny sell,
  My jo Janet.

Keeking in the draw-well clear,
    What if I fhould fa' in?
Syne a' my kin will fay and fwear,
    I drown'd myfell for fin.
Had the better be the brae,
    Janet, Janet;
Had the better be the brae,
    My jo Janet.

Good Sir, for your courtefie,
    Coming through Aberdeen then,
For the love ye bear to me,
    Buy me a pair of fhoon then.
Clout the auld, the new are dear,
    Janet, Janet;
Ae pair may gain ye ha'f a year,
    My jo Janet.

But what if dancing on the green,
    And fkipping like a mawking,
If they fhould fee my clouted fhoon,
    Of me they will be tauking.
Dance ay laigh, and late at e'en,
    Janet, Janet;
Syne a' their fauts will no be feen,
    My jo Janet.

Kind Sir, for your courtefie,
    When ye gae to the crofs then,
For the love ye bear to me,
    Buy me a pacing horfe then.
Pace upo' your fpinning-wheel,
    Janet, Janet;
Pace upo' your fpinning-wheel,
    My jo Janet.

My fpinning-wheel is auld and ftiff,
    The rock o't winna ftand, Sir,

To keep the temper-pin in tiff,
  Employs aft my hand, Sir.
Make the beſt o't that ye can,
  Janet, Janet;
But like it never wale a man,
  My jo Janet.

SONG.

Tune—*John Anderſon my jo.*

WHAT means this niceneſs now of late,
  Since time that truth does prove;
Such diſtance may conſiſt with ſtate,
  But never will with love.
'Tis either cunning or diſdain
  That does ſuch ways allow;
The firſt is baſe, the laſt is vain:
  May neither happen you.

For if it be to draw me on,
  You over-act your part;
And if it be to have me gone,
  You need not ha'f that art:
For if you chance a look to caſt,
  That ſeems to be a frown,
I'll give you all the love that's paſt,
  The reſt ſhall be my own.

Auld Rob Morris.

MITHER.

AULD Rob Morris that wins in yon glen, [men,
  He's the king of good fellows, and wale of auld
Has fourſcore of black ſheep, and fourſcore too;
Auld Rob Morris is the man ye maun loo.

Doughter.

Had your tongue, mither, and let that abee,
For his eild and my eild can never agree:
They'll never agree, and that will be seen;
For he is fourscore, and I'm but fifteen.

Mither.

Had your tongue, doughter, and lay by your pride,
For he's be the bridegroom, and ye's be the bride:
He shall ly by your side, and kifs ye too;
Auld Rob Morris is the man ye maun loo.

Doughter.

Auld Rob Morris I ken him fou weel,
His a—— it sticks out like ony peat-creel,
He's outshinn'd, inkneed, and ringle-ey'd too;
Auld Rob Morris is the man I'll ne'er loo.

Mither.

Though auld Rob Morris be an elderly man,
Yet his auld brass it will buy a new pan;
Then, doughter, ye should na be so ill to shoo,
For auld Rob Morris is the man ye maun loo.

Doughter.

But auld Rob Morris I never will hae,
His back is sae stiff, and his beard is grown gray:
I had titter die than live wi' him a year;
Sae mair of Rob Morris I never will hear.   Q.

SONG.

Tune—*Come kifs with me, come clap with me,* &c.

Peggy.

My Jocky blyth, for what thou'st done,
   There is nae help nor mending;
For thou hast jogg'd me out of tune,
   For a' thy fair pretending.

My mither sees a change on me,
    For my complexion dashes;
And this, alas! has been with thee
    Sae late amang the rashes.

JOCKY.

My Peggy, what I've said I'll do,
    To free thee frae her scouling.
Come then and let us buckle to,
    Nae langer let's be fooling;
For her content I'll instant wed,
    Since thy complexion dashes;
And then we'll try a feather-bed,
    'Tis safter than the rashes.

PEGGY.

Then, Jocky, since thy love's sae true,
    Let mither scoul, I'm easy:
Sae lang's I live I ne'er shall rue
    For what I've done to please thee.
And there's my hand, I's ne'er complain:
    Oh! weel's me on the rashes;
Whene'er thou likes I'll do't again,
    And a fig for a' their clashes.   Z.

SONG.

Tune—*Rothes's lament;* or, *Pinky-house.*

AS Sylvia in a forest lay,
    To vent her wo alone;
Her swain Sylvander came that way,
    And heard her dying moan:
Ah! is my love (she said) to you
    So worthless and so vain?
Why is your wonted fondness now
    Converted to disdain?

You vow'd the light fhould darknefs turn,
   Ere you'd exchange your love;
In fhades now may creation mourn,
   Since you unfaithful prove.
Was it for this I credit gave
   To ev'ry oath you fwore?
But ah! it feems they moft deceive,
   Who moft our charms adore.

'Tis plain your drift was all deceit,
   The practice of mankind:
Alas! I fee it, but too late,
   My love had made me blind.
For you, delighted I could die:
   But oh! with grief I'm fill'd,
To think that credulous conftant I
   Shou'd by yourfelf be kill'd.

This faid—all breathlefs, fick, and pale,
   Her head upon her hand,
She found her vital fpirits fail,
   And fenfes at a ftand.
Sylvander then began to melt:
   But ere the word was given,
The heavy hand of death fhe felt,
   And figh'd her foul to heaven.   M.

The young LAIRD and EDINBURGH KATY.

NOW wat ye wha I met yeftreen,
   Coming down the ftreet, my jo?
My miftrefs in her tartan fcreen,
   Fu' bonny, braw, and fweet, my jo.
My dear, quoth I, thanks to the night,
   That never wifh'd a lover ill,

Since ye're out of your mother's fight,
  Let's tak a wauk up to the hill.

O Katy, wiltu' gang wi' me,
  And leave the dinfome town a while;
The bloſſom's ſprouting frae the tree,
  And a' the fimmer's gaw'n to fmile:
The mavis, nightingale, and lark,
  The bleating lambs, and whiſtling hind,
In ilka dale, green, fhaw, and park,
  Will nouriſh health, and glad ye'r mind.

Soon as the clear goodman of day
  Bends his morning draught of dew,
We'll gae to fome burn-fide and play,
  And gather flow'rs to buſk ye'r brow;
We'll pou the daifies on the green,
  The lucken gowans frae the bog:
Between hands now and then we'll lean,
  And fport upo' the velvet fog.

There's up into a pleafant glen,
  A wee piece frae my father's tow'r,
A canny, faft, and flow'ry den,
  Which circling birks have form'd a bow'r:
Whene'er the fun grows high and warm,
  We'll to the cauler fhade remove,
There will I lock thee in mine arm,
  And love and kifs, and kifs and love.

Katy's Anſwer.

MY mither's ay glowran o'er me,
  Tho' fhe did the fame before me:
    I canna get leave
    To look to my loove,
Or elfe fhe'll be like to devour me.

Right fain wad I tak ye'r offer,
Sweet Sir, but I'll tine my tocher;
    Then, Sandy, ye'll fret,
    And wyte ye'r poor Kate,
Whene'er ye keek in your toom coffer.

For tho' my father has plenty
Of filler and plenifhing dainty,
    Yet he's unco fweer
    To twin wi' his gear;
And fae we had need to be tenty.

Tutor my parents wi' caution,
Be wylie in ilka motion;
    Brag well o' ye'r land,
    And there's my leal hand,
Win them, I'll be at your devotion.

MARY SCOT.

HAPPY'S the love which meets return,
    When in foft flames fouls equal burn;
But words are wanting to difcover
The torments of a hopelefs lover.
Ye regifters of heav'n, relate,
If looking o'er the rolls of fate,
Did you there fee me mark'd to marrow
Mary Scot the flow'r of Yarrow?

  Ah no! her form's too heav'nly fair,
Her love the gods above muft fhare;
While mortals with defpair explore her,
And at diftance due adore her.
O lovely maid! my doubts beguile,
Revive and blefs me with a fmile:
Alas! if not, you'll foon debar a
Sighing fwain the banks of Yarrow.

Be hufh, ye fears, I'll not defpair;
My Mary's tender as fhe's fair;
Then I'll go tell her all mine anguifh,
She is too good to let me languifh:
With fuccefs crown'd, I'll not envy
The folks who dwell above the fky;
When Mary Scot's become my marrow,
We'll make a paradife in Yarrow.

O'er Bogie.

I WILL awa' wi' my love,
    I will awa' wi' her,
Tho' a' my kin had fworn and faid,
    I'll o'er Bogie wi' her.
If I can get but her confent,
    I dinna care a ftrae;
Tho' ilka ane be difcontent,
    Awa' wi' her I'll gae.
I will awa', &c.

For now fhe's miftrefs of my heart,
    And wordy of my hand,
And well I wat we fhanna part
    For filler or for land.
Let rakes delyte to fwear and drink,
    And beaus admire fine lace,
But my chief pleafure is to blink
    On Betty's bonny face.
I will awa', &c.

There a' the beauties do combine,
    Of colour, treats, and air,
The faul that fparkles in her een
    Makes her a jewel rare:

Her flowing wit gives ſhining life
    To a' her other charms;
How bleſs'd I'll be when ſhe's my wife,
    And lock'd up in my arms!
I will awa', &c.

There blythly will I rant and ſing,
    While o'er her ſweets I range,
I'll cry, Your humble ſervant, King,
    Shame fa' them that wad change.
A kiſs of Betty and a ſmile,
    A'beit ye wad lay down
The right ye hae to Britain's iſle,
    And offer me ye'r crown.
I will awa', &c.

O'er the Moor to MAGGY.

AND I'll o'er the moor to Maggy,
    Her wit and ſweetneſs call me;
Then to my fair I'll ſhow my mind,
    Whatever may befal me.
If ſhe love mirth, I'll learn to ſing;
    Or likes the Nine to follow,
I'll lay my lugs in Pindus' ſpring,
    And invocate Apollo.

If ſhe admire a martial mind,
    I'll ſheath my limbs in armour;
If to the ſofter dance inclin'd,
    With gayeſt airs I'll charm her:
If ſhe love grandeur, day and night,
    I'll plot my nation's glory,
Find favour in my prince's ſight,
    And ſhine in future ſtory.

Beauty can wonders work with eafe,
　　Where wit is correfponding;
And bravest men know beft to pleafe,
　　With complaifance abounding.
My bonny Maggy's love can turn
　　Me to what fhape fhe pleafes,
If in her breaft that flame fhall burn,
　　Which in my bofom blazes.

Polwart on the Green.

*AT Polwart on the Green
　　If you'll meet me the morn,
Where laffes do convene
　　To dance about the thorn,*
A kindly welcome you fhall meet
　　Frae her wha likes to view
A lover and a lad complete,
　　The lad and lover you.

Let dorty dames fay *Na*,
　　As lang as e'er they pleafe,
Seem caulder than the fna',
　　While inwardly they bleeze;
But I will frankly fhaw my mind,
　　And yield my heart to thee;
Be ever to the captive kind,
　　That langs na to be free.

At Polwart on the green,
　　Amang the new-mawn hay,
With fangs and dancing keen
　　We'll pafs the heartfome day.
*At night, if beds be o'er thrang laid,
　　And thou be twin'd of thine,
Thou fhalt be welcome, my dear lad,
　　To take a part of mine.*

John Hay's Bonny Laſſie.

BY ſmooth winding Tay a ſwain was reclining,
    Aft cry'd he, Oh hey! maun I ſtill live pining
Myſell thus away, and darna diſcover
To my bonny Hay that I am her lover?

    Nae mair it will hide, the flame waxes ſtranger:
If ſhe's not my bride, my days are na langer:
Then I'll take a heart, and try at a venture,
May be, ere we part, my vows may content her.

    She's freſh as the ſpring, and ſweet as Aurora,
When birds mount and ſing, bidding day a good mor-
The ſward of the mead, enamel'd with daiſies, [row.
Look wither'd and dead, when twin'd of her graces.

    But if ſhe appear where verdures invite her,
The fountains run clear, and flow'rs ſmell the ſweeter:
'Tis heaven to be by, when her wit is a-flowing,
Her ſmiles and bright eye ſet my ſpirits a-glowing.

    The mair that I gaze the deeper I'm wounded;
Struck dumb with amaze, my mind is confounded:
I'm all on a fire, dear maid, to careſs ye,
For a' my deſire is Hay's bonny laſſie.

Katharine Ogie.

AS walking forth to view the plain,
    Upon a morning early,
While May's ſweet ſcent did chear my brain,
    From flow'rs which grew ſo rarely:
I chanc'd to meet a pretty maid,
    She ſhin'd, though it was foggy;
I aſk'd her name: Sweet Sir, ſhe ſaid,
    My name is Katharine Ogie.

I stood a while, and did admire,
    To see a nymph so stately;
So brisk an air there did appear
    In a country-maid so neatly:
Such natural sweetness she display'd,
    Like a lilie in a boggie;
Diana's self was ne'er array'd
    Like this same Katharine Ogie.

Thou flow'r of females, beauty's queen,
    Who sees thee, sure must prize thee;
Though thou art dress'd in robes but mean,
    Yet these cannot disguise thee;
Thy handsome air, and graceful look,
    Far excels any clownish rogie;
Thou'rt match for laird, or lord, or duke,
    My charming Katharine Ogie.

O were I but some shepherd swain!
    To feed my flock beside thee,
At boughting time to leave the plain,
    In milking to abide thee;
I'd think myself a happier man,
    With Kate, my club, and dogie,
Than he that hugs his thousands ten,
    Had I but Katharine Ogie.

Then I'd despise th' imperial throne,
    And statesmen's dang'rous stations:
I'd be no King, I'd wear no crown,
    I'd smile at conq'ring nations:
Might I caress and still possess
    This lass of whom I'm vogie;
For these are toys, and still look less,
    Compar'd with Katharine Ogie.

But I fear the gods have not decreed
    For me so fine a creature,
Whose beauty rare makes her exceed
    All other works in nature.

Clouds of despair surround my love,
  That are both dark and foggy:
Pity my case, ye powers above,
  Else I die for Katharine Ogie.

An thou were my ain Thing.

OF race divine thou needs must be,
  Since nothing earthly equals thee;
For heaven's sake, oh! favour me,
  Who only lives to love thee.
    An thou were my ain thing,
    I would love thee, I would love thee;
    An thou were my ain thing,
    How dearly would I love thee!

The gods one thing peculiar have,
To ruin none whom they can save;
O! for their sake support a slave,
  Who only lives to love thee.
    An thou were, &c.

To merit I no claim can make,
But that I love, and for your sake,
What man can name I'll undertake,
  So dearly do I love thee.
    An thou were, &c.

My passion, constant as the sun,
Flames stronger still, will ne'er have done
Till fates my thread of life have spun,
  Which breathing out I'll love thee.
    An thou were, &c.

* * * * * * * * *

Like bees that fuck the morning dew,
Frae flowers of fweetest scent and hew,
Sae wad I dwell upo' thy mou'
   And gar the gods envy me.
     An thou were, &c.

Sae lang's I had the ufe of light,
I'd on thy beauties feaft my fight,
Syne in faft whifpers through the night,
   I'd tell how much I loo'd thee.
     An thou were, &c.

How fair and ruddy is my Jean!
She moves a goddefs o'er the green;
Were I a king, thou fhould be queen,
   Nane but myfell aboon thee.
     An thou were, &c.

I'd grafp thee to this breaft of mine,
Whilft thou, like ivy, or the vine,
Around my ftronger limbs fhou'd twine,
   Form'd hardy to defend thee.
     An thou were, &c.

Time's on the wing, and will not ftay,
In fhining youth let's make our hay;
Since love admits of nae delay,
   O let nae fcorn undo thee.
     An thou were, &c.

While Love does at his altar ftand,
Hae there's my heart, gi'e me thy hand,
And, with ilk fmile, thou fhalt command
   The will of him wha loves thee.
     An thou were, &c.

There's my Thumb I'll ne'er beguile thee.

MY sweetest May, let love incline thee,
  T" accept a heart which he designs thee;
And, as your constant slave, regard it,
Syne for its faithfulness reward it.
'Tis proof a-shot to birth or money,
But yields to what is sweet and bonny;
Receive it then with a kiss and a smily,
There's my thumb 'twill ne'er beguile ye.

How tempting sweet these lips of thine are,
Thy bosom white, and legs sae fine are,
That, when in pools I see thee clean 'em,
They carry away my heart between 'em.
I wish, and I wish, while it gaes duntin,
O gin I had thee on a mountain,
Though kith and kin and a' shou'd revile thee,
There's my thumb I'll ne'er beguile thee.

Alane through flow'ry hows I dander,
Tenting my flocks lest they shou'd wander,
Gin thou'll gae alang, I'll dawt thee gaylie,
And gi'e my thumb I'll ne'er beguile thee.
O my dear lassie, it is but daffin,
To had thy wooer up ay niff-naffin.
That na, na, na, I hate it most vilely,
O say Yes, and I'll ne'er beguile thee.

For the Love of JEAN.

JOCKY said to Jeany, Jeany, wilt thou do't?
  Ne'er a fit, quo' Jeany, for my tocher-good,
For my tocher-good, I winna marry thee.
E'ens ye like, quo' Jonny, ye may let it be.

I hae gowd and gear, I hae land enough,
I hae feven good owfen ganging in a pleugh,
Ganging in a pleugh, and linking o'er the lee,
And gin ye winna tak me, I can let ye be.

I hae a good ha' houfe, a barn and a byre,
A ftack afore the door, I'll make a rantin fire,
I'll make a rantin fire, and merry fhall we be:
And gin ye winna tak me, I can let ye be.

Jeany faid to Jocky, Gin ye winna tell,
Ye fhall be the lad, I'll be the lafs myfell.
Ye're a bonny lad, and I'm a laffie free,
Ye're welcomer to tak me than to let me be.   Z.

✣✣✣

SONG.

Tune—*Peggy, I muft love thee.*

BENEATH a beech's grateful fhade,
 Young Colin lay complaining;
He figh'd, and feem'd to love a maid,
 Without hopes of obtaining:
For thus the fwain indulg'd his grief,
 Though pity cannot move thee,
Though thy hard heart gives no relief,
 Yet, Peggy, I muft love thee.

Say, Peggy, what has Colin done,
 That thus you cruelly ufe him?
If love's a fault, 'tis that alone
 For which you fhould excufe him.
'Twas thy dear felf firft rais'd this flame,
 This fire by which I languifh;
'Tis thou alone can quench the fame,
 And cool its fcorching anguifh.

For thee I leave the fportive plain,
  Where ev'ry maid invites me ;
For thee, fole caufe of all my pain,
  For thee that only flights me :
This love that fires my faithful heart
  By all but thee's commended.
Oh ! would thou act fo good a part,
  My grief might foon be ended.

That beauteous breaft, fo foft to feel,
  Seem'd tendernefs all over,
Yet it defends thy heart like fteel,
  'Gainft thy defpairing lover.
Alas ! tho' fhould it ne'er relent,
  Nor Colin's care e'er move thee,
Yet till life's lateft breath is fpent,
  My Peggy, I muft love thee.   C.

Genty Tibby, and Sonfy Nelly.

Tune—Tibby Fowler in the glen.

TIBBY has a ftore o' charms,
  Her genty fhape our fancy warms ;
How ftrangely can her fma' white arms
  Fetter the lad who looks but at her ?
Fra'er ancle to her flender waift,
  Thefe fweets conceal'd invite to dawt her;
Her rofy cheek, and rifing breaft,
  Gar ane's mouth gufh bowt fu' o' water.

Nelly's gawfy, faft, and gay,
Frefh as the lucken flowers in May;
Ilk ane that fees her, crys, *Ah hey*,
  She's bonny! O I wonder at her !

The dimples of her chin and cheek,
  And limbs sae plump invite to dawt her;
Her lips sae sweet, and skin sae sleek,
  Gar mony mouths beside mine water.

Now strike my finger in a bore,
My wyson with the maiden shore,
Gin I can tell whilk I am for,
  When these twa stars appear the gither.
O love! why dost thou gi'e thy fires
  Sae large, while we're obliged to nither
Our spacious fauls immense desires,
  And ay be in a hankerin swither.

Tibby's shape and airs are fine,
And Nelly's beauties are divine:
But since they canna baith be mine,
  Ye gods, give ear to my petition:
Provide a good lad for the tane;
  But let it be with this provision,
I get the other to my lane,
  In prospect *plano* and fruition.

Up in the Air.

NOW the sun's gane out o' sight,
  Beet the ingle, and snuff the light;
In glens the fairies skip and dance,
And witches wallop o'er to France.
    Up in the air
    On my bonny gray mare,
And I see her yet, and I see her yet.
    Up in, &c.

The wind's drifting hail and sna',
O'er frozen hags, like a foot-ba';
Nae starns keek thro' th' azure flit,
'Tis cauld, and mirk as ony pit.

   The man i' the moon
   Is carousing aboon;
D'ye see, d'ye see, d'ye see him yet?
   The man, &c.

Take your glass to clear your een,
'Tis the elixir heals the spleen,
Baith wit and mirth it will inspire,
And gently puffs the lover's fire.
   Up in the air,
   It drives away care;
Ha'e wi' ye, ha'e wi' ye, and ha'e wi' ye, lads, yet.
   Up in, &c.

Steek the doors, keep out the frost;
Come, Willie, gi's about your toast;
Til't, lads, and lilt it out,
And let us ha'e a blythsome bout.
   Up wi't there, there,
   Dinna cheat, but drink fair:
Huzza, huzza, and huzza, lads, yet.
   Up wi't, &c.

Fy gar rub her o'er wi' Strae.

GIN ye meet a bonny lassie,
 Gi'e her a kiss, and let her gae;
But if ye meet a dirty hussy,
 Fy gar rub her o'er wi' strae.

Be sure ye dinna quit the grip
 Of ilka joy, when ye are young,
Before auld age your vitals nip,
 And lay ye twafald o'er a rung.

Sweet youth's a blyth and heartsome time:
 Then, lads and lasses, while 'tis May,
Gae pu' the gowan in its prime,
 Before it wither and decay.

Watch the faft minutes of delyte,
  When Jenny fpeaks beneath her breath,
And kiffes, laying a' the wyte
  On you, if fhe kepp ony fkaith.

Haith ye're ill-bred, fhe'll fmiling fay,
  Ye'll worry me, ye greedy rook:
Syne frae your arms fhe'll rin away,
  And hide herfelf in fome dark nook.

Her laugh will lead you to the place
  Where lies the happinefs you want,
And plainly tell you to your face,
  Nineteen na-fays are ha'f a grant.

Now to her heaving bofom cling,
  And fweetly toolie for a kifs:
Frae her fair finger whoop a ring,
  As taiken of a future blifs.

Thefe bennifons, I'm very fure,
  Are of the gods indulgent grant:
Then, furly carls, whifht, forbear
  To plague us with your whining cant.

Patie and Peggy.

Patie.

BY the delicious warmnefs of thy mouth,
  And rowing eye, which fmiling tells the truth,
I guefs, my laffie, that, as well as I,
You're made for love, and why fhould ye deny?

Peggy.

But ken ye, lad, gin we confefs o'er foon,
Ye think us cheap, and fyne the wooing's done:
The maiden that o'er quickly tines her pow'r,
Like unripe fruit, will tafte but hard and four.

Patie.

But when they hing o'er lang upon the tree,
Their sweetness they may tine, and sae may ye:
Red-cheeked you completely ripe appear,
And I have thol'd and woo'd a lang ha'f-year.

Peggy.

Then dinna pu' me; gently thus I fa'
Into my Patie's arms for good and a':
But stint your wishes to this frank embrace,
And mint nae farther till we've got the grace.

Patie.

O charming armfu'! hence, ye cares, away,
I'll kiss my treasure a' the live-lang day:
A' night I'll dream my kisses o'er again,
Till that day come that ye'll be a' my ain.

Chorus.

Sun, gallop down the westlin skies,
Gang soon to bed and quickly rise:
O lash your steeds, post time away,
And haste about our bridal-day:
And if ye're weary'd, honest light,
Sleep gin ye like a week that night.

The Mill, Mill—O.

BENEATH a green shade I fand a fair maid,
    Was sleeping sound and still—O;
A' lowan wi' love, my fancy did rove
    Around her with good will—O:
Her bosom I press'd; but sunk in her rest,
    She stirr'dna my joy to spill—O:
While kindly she slept, close to her I crept,
    And kiss'd, and kiss'd her my fill—O.

Oblig'd by command in Flanders to land,
  T' employ my courage and fkill—O,
Frae her quietly I ftaw, hoift fails and awa',
  For the wind blew fair on the bill—O.
Twa years brought me hame, where loud-fraifing fame
  Tald me with a voice right fhrill—O,
My lafs, like a fool, had mounted the ftool,
  Nor kend wha had done her the ill—O.

Mair fond of her charms, with my fon in her arms,
  I ferlying fpeer'd how fhe fell—O.
Wi' the tear in her eye, quoth fhe, Let me die,
  Sweet Sir, gin I can tell—O.
Love gave the command, I took her by the hand,
  And bade her a' fears expel—O,
And nae mair look wan, for I was the man
  Wha had done her the deed myfell—O.

My bonny fweet lafs, on the gowany grafs,
  Beneath the Shilling-hill—O,
If I did offence, I'fe make ye amends
  Before I leave Peggy's mill—O.
O the mill, mill—O, and the kill, kill—O,
  And the coggin of the wheel—O:
The fack and the fieve, a' that ye maun leave,
  And round with a fodger reel—O.

☙☙☙☙☙☙☙☙☙☙☙☙☙☙☙☙☙☙☙☙☙☙☙☙☙☙☙☙☙

Colin and Grisy parting.

Tune—*Wo's my heart that we fhould funder.*

WITH broken words, and downcaft eyes,
  Poor Colin fpoke his paffion tender;
And, parting with his Grify, cries,
  Ah! wo's my heart that we fhould funder.

To others I am cold as fnow,
   But kindle with thine eyes like tinder;
From thee with pain I'm forc'd to go:
   It breaks my heart that we fhould funder.

Chain'd to thy charms, I cannot range,
   No beauty new my love fhall hinder,
Nor time nor place fhall ever change
   My vows, though we're oblig'd to funder.

The image of thy graceful air,
   And beauties which invite our wonder,
Thy lively wit and prudence rare,
   Shall ftill be prefent, though we funder.

Dear nymph, believe thy fwain in this,
   You'll ne'er engage a heart that's kinder;
Then feal a promife with a kifs,
   Always to love me though we funder.

Ye gods, take care of my dear lafs,
   That as I leave her I may find her,
When that blefs'd time fhall come to pafs,
   We'll meet again, and never funder.

The Gaberlunzie-man.

THE pawky auld carle came o'er the lee,
   Wi' mony good e'ens and days to me,
Saying, Goodwife, for your courtefie,
   Will you lodge a filly poor man?
The night was cauld, the carl was wat,
And down ayont the ingle he fat;
My doughter's fhoulders he 'gan to clap,
   And cadgily ranted and fang.

O wow! quo' he, were I as free
As firſt when I ſaw this country,
How blyth and merry wad I be!
 And I wad never think lang.
He grew canty, and ſhe grew fain;
But little did her auld minny ken
What thir flee twa togither were ſay'ng,
 When wooing they were ſae thrang.

And O! quo' he, an ye were as black
As e'er the crown of my daddy's hat,
'Tis I wad lay thee by my back,
 And awa' wi' me thou ſhou'd gang.
And O! quo' ſhe, an I were as white
As e'er the ſnaw lay on the dike,
I'd clead me braw and lady-like,
 And awa' with thee I wou'd gang.

Between the twa was made a plot;
They raiſe a wee before the cock,
And wilily they ſhot the lock,
 And faſt to the bent are gane.
Up in the morn the auld wife raiſe,
And at her leiſure put on her claiſe,
Syne to the ſervant's bed ſhe gaes,
 To ſpeer for the ſilly poor man.

She gaed to the bed where the beggar lay,
The ſtrae was cauld, he was away,
She clapt her hand, cry'd, Waladay,
 For ſome of our gear will be gane.
Some ran to coffers and ſome to kiſts,
But nought was flown that cou'd be miſt;
She danc'd her lane, cry'd, Praiſe be bleſt,
 I have lodg'd a leal poor man.

Since naething's awa', as we can learn,
The kirn's to kirn, and milk to earn,
Gae but the houſe, laſs, and waken my bairn,
 And bid her come quickly ben.

G

The fervant gaed where the doughter lay,
The fheets were cauld, fhe was away,
And faft to her goodwife did fay,
    She's aff with the Gaberlunzie-man.

O fy gar ride, and fy gar rin,
And hafte ye find thefe traitors again;
For fhe's be burnt, and he's be flain,
    The wearifu' Gaberlunzie-man.
Some rade upo' horfe, fome ran a-fit,
The wife was wood, and out o' her wit:
She cou'd na gang, nor yet cou'd fhe fit,
    But ay fhe curs'd and fhe bann'd.

Mean time far hind out o'er the lee,
Fu' fnug in a glen, where nane cou'd fee,
The twa, with kindly fport and glee,
    Cut frae a new cheefe a whang:
The priving was good, it pleas'd them baith,
To lo'e her for ay, he gae her his aith,
Quo' fhe, to leave thee I will be laith,
    My winfome Gaberlunzie-man.

O kend my minny I were wi' you,
Ill-fardly wad fhe crook her mou',
Sic a poor man fhe'd never trow,
    After the Gaberlunzie-man.
My dear, quo' he, ye're yet o'er young,
And hae nae learn'd the beggar's tongue,
To follow me frae town to town,
    And carry the Gaberlunzie on.

Wi' cauk and keel I'll win your bread,
And fpindles and whorles for them wha need,
Whilk is a gentle trade indeed,
    To carry the Gaberlunzie on.
I'll bow my leg, and crook my knee,
And draw a black clout o'er my eye,
A cripple or blind they will ca' me,
    While we fhall be merry and fing.   I.

THE CORDIAL.

Tune—*Where shall our goodman lie?*

HE.

WHERE wad bonny Annie lie?
    Alane nae mair ye maun lie;
Wad ye a goodman try?
    Is that the thing ye're lacking!

SHE.

Can a lafs fae young as I
Venture on the bridal-tie,
Syne down with a goodman lie?
    I'm flee'd he keep me wauking.

HE.

Never judge until ye try,
Mak me your goodman, I
Shanna hinder you to lie,
    And fleep till ye be weary.

SHE.

What if I fhou'd wauking lie,
When the hoboys are gawn by,
Will ye tent me when I cry,
    My dear, I'm faint and iry?

HE.

In my bofom thou fhalt lie,
When thou waukrife art, or dry,
Healthy cordial ftanding by,
    Shall prefently revive thee.

SHE.

To your will I then comply,
Join us, Prieft, and let me try
How I'll wi' a goodman lie,
    Wha can a cordial give me.

Ew-Bughts Marion.

WILL ye go to the ew-bughts, Marion,
    And wear in the sheep wi' me?
The sun shines sweet, my Marion,
    But nae half sae sweet as thee.
O Marion's a bonny lass,
    And the blyth blink's in her eye;
And fain wad I marry Marion,
    Gin Marion wad marry me.

There's gowd in your garters, Marion,
    And silk on your white hauss-bane;
Fu' fain wad I kiss my Marion,
    At even when I come hame.
There's braw lads in Earnslaw, Marion,
    Wha gape, and glowr with their eye,
At kirk, when they see my Marion;
    But nane of them lo'es like me.

I've nine milk-ewes, my Marion;
    A cow and a brawny quey,
I'll gi'e them a' to my Marion,
    Just on her bridal-day;
And ye's get a green sey apron,
    And waistcoat of the London brown,
And wow but ye will be vap'ring,
    Whene'er ye gang to the town.

I'm young and stout, my Marion;
    Nane dances like me on the green:
And gin ye forsake me, Marion,
    I'll e'en gae draw up wi' Jean:
Sae put on your pearlins, Marion,
    And kyrtle of the cramasie;
And soon as my chin has nae hair on,
    I shall come west, and see ye.   Q.

The Blythsome Bridal.

FY let us a' to the bridal,
    For there will be lilting there;
For Jocky's to be married to Maggie,
    The lafs wi' the gowden hair.
And there will be lang-kail and pottage,
    And bannocks of barley-meal;
And there will be good fawt herring,
    To relifh a cog of good ale.
Fy let us a' to the bridal, &c.

And there will be Sawney the futor,
    And Will wi' the meikle mou';
And there will be Tam the blutter,
    With Andrew the tinkler, I trow;
And there will be bow-legg'd Robbie,
    With thumblefs Katy's goodman;
And there will be blue-cheeked Dowbie,
    And Lawrie the laird of the land.
Fy let us, &c.

And there will be fow-libber Patie,
    And plucky-fac'd Wat i' the mill,
Caper-nos'd Francie and Gibbie,
    That wins in the how of the hill;
And there will be Alafter Sibbie,
    Wha in with black Beffie did mool,
With fnivelling Lilly and Tibby,
    The lafs that ftands aft on the ftool.
Fy let us, &c.

And Madge that was buckled to Steenie,
    And coft him grey breeks to his arfe,
Who after was hangit for ftealing,
    Great mercy it happen'd na warfe:

And there will be gleed Geordy Janners,
    And Kirſh wi' the lilly-white leg,
Wha gade to the ſouth for manners,
    And bang'd up her wame in Mons-meg.
Fy let us, &c.

And there will be Judan Maclawrie,
    And blinkin daft Barbara Macleg,
Wi' flae-lugged ſharney-fac'd Lawrie,
    And ſhangy-mou'd haluket Meg.
And there will be happer-ars'd Nanſy,
    And fairy-fac'd Flowrie by name,
Muck Madie, and fat-hippit Griſy,
    The laſs wi' the gowden wame.
Fy let us, &c.

And there will be Girn-again-Gibbie,
    With his glaikit wife Jenny Bell,
And miſle-ſhinn'd Mungo Macapie,
    The lad that was ſkipper himſell.
There lads and laſſes in pearlings
    Will feaſt in the heart of the ha',
On ſybows, and riſarts, and carlings,
    That are baith ſodden and raw.
Fy let us, &c.

And there will be fadges and brachan,
    With fowth of good gabbocks of ſkate,
Powſowdy, and drammock, and crowdy,
    And cauler nowt-feet in a plate:
And there will be partans and buckies,
    And whitens and ſpeldings enew,
With ſinged ſheep-heads, and a haggies,
    And ſcadlips to ſup till ye ſpew.
Fy let us, &c.

And there will be lapper'd-milk kebbocks,
    And fowens, and farls, and baps,
With ſwats, and well-ſcraped paunches,
    And brandy in ſtoups and in caps:

And there will be meal-kail and caſtocks,
  With ſkink to ſup till ye rive,
And roaſts to roaſt on a brander,
  Of flowks that were taken alive.
Fy let us, &c.

Scrapt haddocks, wilks, dulſe and tangle,
  And a mill of good ſniſhing to prie;
When weary with eating and drinking,
  We'll riſe up and dance till we die.
Then fy let us a' to the bridal,
  For there will be lilting there;
For Jocky's to be married to Maggie,
  The laſs wi' the gowden hair.   Z.

The Highland Laddie.

THE lawland lads think they are fine;
  But O they're vain and idly gaudy!
How much unlike that gracefu' mien,
  And manly looks of my highland laddie?
O my bonny, bonny highland laddie,
My handſome, charming highland laddie;
May heaven ſtill guard, and love reward
Our lawland laſs and her highland laddie.

If I were free at will to chuſe
  To be the wealthieſt lawland lady,
I'd take young Donald without trews,
  With bonnet blew, and belted plaidy.
O my bonny, &c.

The braweſt beau in borrows-town,
  In a' his airs, with art made ready,
Compar'd to him, he's but a clown;
  He's finer far in's tartan plaidy.
O my bonny, &c.

O'er benty hill with him I'll run,
    And leave my lawland kin and dady;
Frae winter's cauld, and fummer's fun,
    He'll fcreen me with his highland plaidy.
O my bonny, &c.

A painted room, and filken bed,
    May pleafe a lawland laird and lady;
But I can kifs, and be as glad,
    Behind a bufh in's highland plaidy.
O my bonny, &c.

Few compliments between us pafs,
    I ca' him my dear highland laddie,
And he ca's me his lawland lafs,
    Syne rows me in beneath his plaidy.
O my bonny, &c.

Nae greater joy I'll e'er pretend,
    Than that his love prove true and fteady,
Like mine to him, which ne'er fhall end,
    While heaven preferves my highland laddie.
O my bonny, &c.

ALLAN WATER.

Or, My Love ANNIE's very bonny.

WHAT numbers fhall the mufe repeat?
    What verfe be found to praife my Annie?
On her ten thoufand graces wait,
    Each fwain admires, and owns fhe's bonny.
Since firft fhe trod the happy plain,
    She fet each youthful heart on fire;
Each nymph does to her fwain complain,
    That Annie kindles new defire.

This lovely darling deareſt care,
    This new delight, this charming Annie,
Like ſummer's dawn, ſhe's freſh and fair,
    When Flora's fragrant breezes fan ye.
All day the am'rous youths conveen,
    Joyous they ſport and play before her;
All night, when ſhe no more is ſeen,
    In bliſsful dreams they ſtill adore her.

Among the crowd Amyntor came,
    He look'd, he lov'd, he bow'd to Annie;
His riſing ſighs expreſs his flame,
    His words were few, his wiſhes many.
With ſmiles the lovely maid reply'd,
    Kind ſhepherd, why ſhould I deceive ye?
Alas! your love muſt be deny'd,
    This deſtin'd breaſt can ne'er relieve ye.

Young Damon came with Cupid's art,
    His wiles, his ſmiles, his charms beguiling,
He ſtole away my virgin heart;
    Ceaſe, poor Amyntor, ceaſe bewailing.
Some brighter beauty you may find,
    On yonder plain the nymphs are many;
Then chuſe ſome heart that's unconfin'd,
    And leave to Damon his own Annie.   C.

The Collier's Bonny Laſſie.

THE collier has a daughter,
    And O ſhe's wonder bonny;
A laird he was that ſought her,
    Rich baith in lands and money:
The tutors watch'd the motion
    Of this young honeſt lover;
But love is like the ocean;
    Wha can its depth diſcover?

He had the art to pleafe ye,
  And was by a' refpected;
His airs fat round him eafy,
  Genteel, but unaffected.
The collier's bonny laffie,
  Fair as the new-blown lillie,
Ay fweet, and never faucy,
  Secur'd the heart of Willie.

He lov'd beyond expreffion
  The charms that were about her,
And panted for poffeffion,
  His life was dull without her.
After mature refolving,
  Clofe to his breaft he held her,
In fafteft flames diffolving,
  He tenderly thus tell'd her:

My bonny collier's daughter,
  Let naething difcompofe ye,
'Tis no your fcanty tocher
  Shall ever gar me lofe ye:
For I have gear in plenty,
  And love fays, 'Tis my duty
To ware what heav'n has lent me
  Upon your wit and beauty.

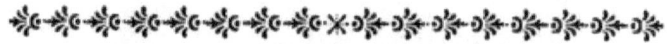

Where Helen lies.

To —— in mourning.

AH! why thofe tears in Nelly's eyes?
    To hear thy tender fighs and cries,
The gods ftand lift'ning from the fkies,
    Pleas'd with thy piety.

To mourn the dead, dear nymph, forbear,
And of one dying take a care,
Who views thee as an angel fair,
    Or some divinity.

O be less graceful, or more kind,
And cool this fever of my mind,
Caus'd by the boy fevere and blind;
    Wounded, I sigh for thee;
While hardly dare I hope to rise
To such a height by Hymen's ties,
To lay me down where Helen lies,
    And with thy charms be free.

Then must I hide my love, and die,
When such a soveregn cure is by?
No; she can love, and I'll go try,
    Whate'er my fate may be;
Which soon I'll read in her bright eyes,
With those dear agents I'll advise,
They tell the truth when tongues tell lies,
    The least believ'd by me.

SONG.

Tune—*Gallowshiels.*

AH the shepherd's mournful fate,
    When doom'd to love, and doom'd to languish,
To bear the scornful fair one's hate,
    Nor dare disclose his anguish.
Yet eager looks, and dying sighs,
    My secret soul discover,
While rapture trembling through mine eyes,
    Reveals how much I love her;

The tender glance, the redd'ning cheek,
   O'erspread with rising blushes,
A thousand various ways they speak
   A thousand various wishes.

For oh! that form so heavenly fair,
   Those languid eyes so sweetly smiling,
That artless blush, and modest air,
   So fatally beguiling.
Thy every look, and every grace,
   So charm whene'er I view thee;
Till death o'ertake me in the chace,
   Still will my hopes pursue thee.
Then when my tedious hours are past,
   Be this last blessing given,
Low at thy feet to breathe my last,
   And die in sight of heaven.

To L. M. M.

Tune—*Rantin roaring Willie.*

O MARY! thy graces and glances,
   Thy smiles so enchantingly gay,
And thoughts so divinely harmonious,
   Clear wit and good humour display.
But say not thou'lt imitate angels
   Ought fairer, though scarcely, ah me!
Can be found equalizing thy merit,
   A match amongst mortals for thee.

Thy many fair beauties shed fires
   May warm up ten thousand to love,
Who despairing, may fly to some other,
   While I may despair, but ne'er rove.

What a mixture of sighing and joys
    This diſtant adoring of thee,
Gives to a fond heart too aſpiring,
    Who loves in ſad ſilence like me?

Thus looks the poor beggar on treaſure,
    And ſhipwreck'd, on landſcapes on ſhore:
Be ſtill more divine and have pity;
    I die ſoon as hope is no more.
For, Mary, my ſoul is thy captive,
    Nor love, nor expects to be free;
Thy beauties are fetters delightful,
    Thy ſlav'ry's a pleaſure to me.

This is no mine ain Houſe.

THIS is not mine ain houſe,
    I ken by the rigging o't;
Since with my love I've changed vows,
    I dinna like the bigging o't.
For now that I'm young Robie's bride,
And miſtreſs of his fire-ſide,
Mine ain houſe I like to guide,
    And pleaſe me with the trigging o't.

Then farewell to my father's houſe,
    I gang where love invites me;
The stricteſt duty this allows,
    When love with honour meets me.
When Hymen moulds us into ane,
My Robie's nearer than my kin,
And to refuſe him were a ſin,
    Sae lang's he kindly treats me.

When I'm in mine ain houſe,
    True love ſhall be at hand ay,
To make me ſtill a prudent ſpouſe,
    And let my man command ay;

Avoiding ilka caufe of ftrife,
The common peft of married life,
That makes ane wearied of his wife,
 And breaks the kindly band ay.

❦❦❦❦❦❦❦❦❦❦❦❦❦❦❦❦❦❦❦❦❦❦❦❦❦❦❦❦❦❦

Fint a Crum of thee fhe faws.

RETURN hameward, my heart, again,
 And bide where thou was wont to be,
Thou art a fool to fuffer pain
 For love of ane that loves not thee.
 My heart, let be fic fantafie,
Love only where thou haft good caufe;
 Since fcorn and liking ne'er agree,
The fint a crum of thee fhe faws.

To what effect fhould thou be thrall?
 Be happy in thine ain free-will,
My heart, be never beftial,
 But ken wha does thee good or ill.
 At hame with me then tarry ftill,
And fee wha can beft play their paws,
 And let the filly fling her fill,
For fint a crum of thee fhe faws.

Though fhe be fair, I will not fenzie,
 She's of a kind with mony mae;
For why, they are a felon menzie
 That feemeth good, and are not fae.
 My heart, take neither flurt nor wae
For Meg, for Marjory, or Maufe,
 But be thou blyth, and let her gae,
For fint a crum of thee she faws.

Remember, how that Medea
 Wild for a fight of Jafon yied,
Remember, how young Creffida
 Left Troilus for Diomede;

Remember Helen, as we read,
Brought Troy from blifs unto bare waws:
   Then let her gae where fhe may fpeed,
For fint a crum of thee fhe faws.

Becaufe fhe faid I took it ill,
   For her depart my heart was fair,
But was beguil'd; gae where fhe will,
   Befhrew the heart that firft takes care:
But be thou merry late and air,
This is the final end and claufe,
   And let her feed and foully fair,
For fint a crum of thee fhe faws.

Ne'er dunt again within my breaft,
   Ne'er let her flights thy courage fpill.
Nor gie a fob, although fhe fneeft,
   She's faireft paid that gets her will.
She gecks as gif I mean'd her ill,
When fhe glaicks paughty in her braws;
   Now let her fnirt and fyke her fill,
For fint a crum of thee fhe faws.   Z.

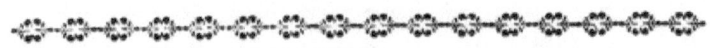

To Mrs. E. C.

Tune—*Sae merry as we have been.*

NOW Phœbus advances on high,
   Nae footfteps of winter are feen;
The birds carrol fweet in the fky,
   And lambkins dance reels on the green.
Through plantings, and burnies fae clear,
   We wander for pleafure and health,
Where buddings and bloffoms appear,
   Giving profpects of joy and wealth.

View ilka gay scene all around,
   That are, and that promise to be;
Yet in them a' naething is found
   Sae perfect, Eliza, as thee.
Thy een the clear fountains excel,
   Thy locks they outrival the grove;
When zephyrs thus pleasingly swell,
   Ilk wave makes a captive to love.

The roses and lilies combin'd,
   And flowers of maist delicate hue,
By thy cheek and dear breasts are outshin'd,
   Their tinctures are naithing sae true.
What can we compare with thy voice,
   And what with thy humour sae sweet?
Nae music can bless with sic joys;
   Sure angels are just sae complete.

Fair blossom of ilka delight,
   Whose beauties ten thousand outshine:
Thy sweet shall be lasting and bright,
   Being mix'd with sae many divine.
Ye pow'rs, who have given sic charms
   To Eliza, your image below,
O save her frae all human harms!
   And make her hours happily flow.

My Daddy forbad, my Minny forbad.

WHEN I think on my lad,
   I sigh and am sad,
For now he is far frae me.
   My daddy was harsh,
   My minny was warse,
That gart him gae yont the sea.

Without an eſtate,
That made him look blate:
And yet a brave lad is he.
Gin fafe he come hame,
In ſpite of my dame,
He'll ever be welcome to me.

Love ſpeers nae advice
Of parents o'er wife,
That have but ae bairn like me,
That looks upon caſh,
As naething but traſh,
That ſhakles what ſhou'd be free.
And though my dear lad
Not ae penny had,
Since qualities better has he;
A'beit I'm an heirefs,
I think it but fair is,
To love him, ſince he loves me.

Then, my dear Jamie,
To thy kind Jeanie,
Haſte, haſte thee in o'er the ſea,
To her wha can find
Nae eaſe in her mind,
Without a blyth fight of thee.
Though my daddy forbad,
And my minny forbad,
Forbidden I will not be;
For ſince thou alone
My favour haſt won,
Nane elſe ſhall e'er get it for me.

Yet them I'll not grieve,
Or without their leave
Gi'e my hand as a wife to thee:
Be content with a heart,
That can never defert,
Till they ceafe to oppofe or be.

My parents may prove
Yet friends to our love,
When our firm refolves they fee;
Then I with pleafure
Will yield up my treafure,
And a' that love orders to thee.

Tune—*Steer her up, and had her gawn.*

O STEER her up, and had her gawn,
　　Her mither's at the mill, jo;
But gin fhe winna tak a man,
　　E'en let her tak her will, jo.
Pray thee, lad, leave filly thinking,
　　Caft thy cares of love away;
Let's our forrows drown in drinking,
'Tis daffin langer to delay.

See that fhining glafs of claret,
　　How invitingly it looks;
Take it aff, and let's hae mair o't,
　　Pox on fighting, trade, and books.
Let's have pleafure while we're able,
　　Bring us in the meikle bowl,
Place't on the middle of the table,
　　And let wind and weather gowl.

Call the drawer, let him fill it
　　Fou, as ever it can hold:
O tak tent ye dinna fpill it,
　　'Tis mair precious far than gold.
By you've drunk a dozen bumpers,
　　Bacchus will begin to prove,
Spite of Venus and her Mumpers,
　　Drinking better is than love.

Clout the Caldron.

HAVE you any pots or pans,
 Or any broken chandlers?
I am a tinkler to my trade,
 And newly come frae Flanders,
As scant of siller as of grace,
 Disbanded, we've a bad run;
Gar tell the lady of the place,
 I'm come to clout her caldron.
Fa adrie, didle, didle, &c.

Madam, if you have wark for me,
 I'll do't to your contentment,
And dinna care a single flie
 For any man's resentment;
For, lady fair, though I appear
 To ev'ry ane a tinkler,
Yet to yoursell I'm bauld to tell,
 I am a gentle jinker.
Fa adrie, didle, didle, &c.

Love Jupiter into a swan
 Turn'd for his lovely Leda;
He like a bull o'er meadows ran,
 To carry aff Europa.
Then may not I, as well as he,
 To cheat your Argos blinker,
And win your love, like mighty Jove,
 Thus hide me in a tinkler?
Fa adrie, didle, didle, &c.

Sir, ye appear a cunning man,
 But this fine plot you'll fail in,
For there is neither pot nor pan
 Of mine you'll drive a nail in.

Then bind your budget on your back,
　　　　And nails up in your apron,
　　　For I've a tinkler under tack
　　　　That's us'd to clout my caldron.
　　　Fa adrie, didle, didle, &c.

The Malt-Man.

THE malt-man comes on Munday,
　　He craves wonder fair,
Cries, *Dame, come gi'e me my filler,*
　　Or malt ye fall ne'er get mair.
I took him into the pantry,
　　And gave him fome good cock-broo,
Syne paid him upon a gantree,
　　As hoftler-wives fhould do.

When malt-men come for filler,
　　And gaugers with wands o'er foon,
Wives, tak them a' down to the cellar,
　　And clear them as I have done.
This bewith, when cunzie is fcanty,
　　Will keep them frae making din;
The knack I learn'd frae an auld aunty,
　　The fnackeft of a' my kin.

The malt-man is right cunning,
　　But I can be as flee,
And he may crack of his winning,
　　When he clears fcores with me:
For come when he likes, I'm ready;
　　But if frae hame I be,
Let him wait on our kind lady,
　　She'll anfwer a bill for me.

Bonny Bessy.

Tune—Bessy's Haggies.

BESSY'S beauties shine sae bright,
    Were her many virtues fewer,
She wad ever give delight,
    And in transport make me view her.
Bonny Bessy, thee alane
    Love I, naething else about thee;
With thy comeliness I'm tane,
    And langer cannot live without thee.

Bessy's bosom's saft and warm,
    Milk-white fingers still employ'd;
He who takes her to his arm,
    Of her sweets can ne'er be cloy'd.
My dear Bessy, when the roses
    Leave thy cheek, as thou grows aulder,
Virtue, which thy mind disclofes,
    Will keep love frae growing caulder.

Bessy's tocher is but scanty.
    Yet her face and soul discovers
These inchanting sweets in plenty
    Must entice a thousand lovers.
'Tis not money, but a woman
    Of a temper kind and easy,
That gives happiness uncommon,
    Petted things can nought but teaze ye.

Omnia vincit Amor.

AS I went forth to view the spring,
    Which Flora had adorned
In raiment fair; now every thing
    The rage of winter scorned:

I caſt mine eye, and did eſpy
   A youth, who made great clamor;
And drawing nigh, I heard him cry,
   Ah! *omnia vincit amor.*

Upon his breaſt he lay along,
   Hard by a murm'ring river,
And mournfully his doleful ſong
   With ſighs he did deliver:
Ah! Jeany's face has comely grace,
   Her locks that ſhine like lammer,
With burning rays have cut my days;
   For *omnia vincit amor.*

Her glancy een like comets ſheen,
   The morning-ſun outſhining,
Have caught my heart in Cupid's net,
   And make me die with pining.
Durſt I complain, nature's to blame,
   So curiouſly to frame her,
Whoſe beauties rare make me with care
   Cry, *Omnia vincit amor.*

Ye cryſtal ſtreams that ſwiftly glide,
   Be partners of my mourning,
Ye fragrant fields and meadows wide,
   Condemn her for her ſcorning:
Let every tree a witneſs be,
   How juſtly I may blame her;
Ye chanting birds, note theſe my words,
   Ah! *omnia vincit amor.*

Had ſhe been kind as ſhe was fair,
   She long had been admired,
And been ador'd for virtues rare,
   Wh' of life now makes me tired.
Thus ſaid, his breath began to fail,
   He could not ſpeak, but ſtammer;
He ſigh'd full ſore, and ſaid no more,
   But *omnia vincit amor.*

When I obferv'd him near to death,
    I run in hafte to fave him,
But quickly he refigned his breath,
    So deep the wound love gave him.
Now for her fake this vow I'll make,
    My tongue fhall ay defame her,
While on his herfe I'll write this verfe,
    Ah! *omnia vincit amor.*

Straight I confider'd in my mind
    Upon the matter rightly,
And found, though Cupid he be blind,
    He proves in pith moft mighty.
For warlike Mars, and thund'ring Jove,
    And Vulcan with his hammer,
Did ever prove the flaves of love,
    For *omnia vincit amor.*

Hence we may fee th' effects of love,
    Which gods and men keep under,
That nothing can his bonds remove,
    Or torments break afunder:
Nor wife, nor fool, need go to fchool,
    To learn this from his grammar;
His heart's the book where he's to look,
    For *omnia vincit amor.*   Q.

The auld Wife beyont the Fire.

I.

THERE was a wife won'd in a glen,
    And fhe had dochters nine or ten,
That fought the houfe baith but and ben,
    To find their mam a fnifhing.
    The auld wife beyont the fire,
    The auld wife aniefl the fire,
    The auld wife aboon the fire,
    She died for lack of fnifhing.

II.

 Her mill into fome hole had fawn,
Whatrecks, quoth fhe, let it be gawn,
For I maun hae a young goodman
  Shall furnifh me with fnifhing.
  The auld wife, &c.

III.

 Her eldeft dochter faid right bauld,
Fy, mother, mind that now ye're auld,
And if ye with a younker wald,
  He'll wafte away your fnifhing.
  The auld wife, &c.

IV.

 The youngeft dochter gae a fhout,
O mother dear! your teeth's a' out,
Befides ha'f blind, you have the gout,
  Your mill can haud nae fnifhing.
  The auld wife, &c.

V.

 Ye lied, ye limmers, cries auld mump,
For I hae baith a tooth and ftump,
And will nae langer live in dump,
  By wanting of my fnifhing.
  The auld wife, &c.

VI.

 Thole ye, fays Peg, that pawky flut,
Mother, if ye can crack a nut,
Then we will a' confent to it,
  That you fhall have a fnifhing.
  The auld wife, &c.

Note—Snifhing, in its literal meaning, is fnuff made of tobacco; but, in this fong, it means fometimes contentment, a hufband, love, money, &c.

VII.

The auld ane did agree to that,
And they a piſtol bullet gat;
She powerfully began to crack,
   To win herſell a ſniſhing.
    The auld wife, &c.

VIII.

Braw ſport it was to ſee her chow't,
And 'tween her gums ſae ſqueez and row't,
While frae her jaws the ſlaver flow'd,
   And ay ſhe curs'd poor ſtumpy.
    The auld wife, &c.

IX.

At laſt ſhe gae a deſperate ſqueez,
Which brak the lang tooth by the neez,
And ſyne poor ſtumpy was at eaſe,
   But ſhe tint hopes of ſniſhing.
    The auld wife, &c.

X.

She of the taſk began to tire,
And frae her dochters did retire,
Syne lean'd her down ayont the fire,
   And died for lack of ſniſhing.
    The auld wife, &c.

XI.

Ye auld wives, notice well this truth,
Aſſoon as ye're paſt mark of mouth,
Ne'er do what's only fit for youth,
   And leave aff thoughts of ſniſhing:
    Elſe, like this wife beyont the fire,
    Ye'r bairns againſt you will conſpire;
    Nor will ye get, unleſs ye hire,
    A young man with your ſniſhing.   Q.

I'll never love thee more.

MY dear and only love, I pray,
    That little world of thee,.
Be govern'd by no other fway,
    But pureſt monarchy:
For if confufion have a part,
    Which virtuous fouls abhor,
I'll call a fynod in my heart,
    And never love thee more.

As Alexander I will reign,
    And I will reign alone,
My thoughts did evermore difdain
    A rival on my throne.
He either fears his fate too much,
    Or his deferts are fmall,
Who dares not put it to the touch,
    To gain or lofe it all.

But I will reign, and govern ſtill,
    And always give the law,
And have each fubject at my will,
    And all to ſtand in awe:
But 'gainſt my batt'ries if I find
    Thou ſtorm or vex me fore,
As if thou fet me as a blind,
    I'll never love thee more.

And in the empire of thy heart,
    Where I fhould folely be,
If others do pretend a part,
    Or dares to fhare with me,
Or committees if thou erect,
    Or go on fuch a fcore,
I'll fmiling, mock at thy neglect,
    And never love thee more.

But if no faithlefs action ftain
 Thy love and conftant word,
I'll make thee famous by my pen,
 And glorious by my fword.
I'll ferve thee in fuch noble ways,
 As ne'er was known before;
I'll deck and crown thy head with bays,
 And love thee more and more.

The Blackbird.

UPON a fair morning, for foft recreation,
 I heard a fair lady was making her moan,
With fighing and fobbing, and fad lamentation,
 Saying, my *blackbird* moft royal is flown.
  My thoughts they deceive me,
  Reflections do grieve me,
And I am o'erburden'd with fad mifery;
  Yet, if death fhould blind me,
  As true love inclines me,
My *blackbird* I'll feek out, wherever he be.

Once in fair England my *blackbird* did flourifh,
 He was the chief flower that in it did fpring;
Prime ladies of honour his perfon did nourifh,
 Becaufe he was the true fon of a king:
  But fince that falfe fortune,
  Which ftill is uncertain,
Has caufed this parting between him and me,
  His name I'll advance
  In Spain and in France,
And feek out my *blackbird* wherever he be.

The birds of the foreft all met together,
 The turtle has chofen to dwell with the dove;
And I am refolv'd, in foul or fair weather,
 Once in the fpring to feek out my love.

He's all my heart's treasure,
My joy and my pleasure;
And justly (my love) my heart follows thee,
Who art constant and kind,
And courageous of mind,
All bliss on my *blackbird* wherever he be.

In England my *blackbird* and I were together,
Where he was still noble and gen'rous of heart;
Ah! wo to the time that first he went thither,
Alas! he was forc'd from thence to depart.
In Scotland he's deem'd,
And highly esteem'd,
In England he seemeth a stranger to be;
Yet his fame shall remain
In France and in Spain;
All bliss to my *blackbird*, wherever he be.

What if the fowler my *blackbird* has taken,
Then sighing and sobbing will be all my tune;
But if he is safe, I'll not be forsaken,
And hope yet to see him in May or in June.
For him through the fire,
Through mud and through mire,
I'll go; for I love him to such a degree,
Who is constant and kind,
And noble of mind,
Deserving all blessings, wherever he be.

It is not the ocean can fright me with danger,
Nor though, like a pilgrim, I wander forlorn,
I may meet with friendship of one is a stranger,
More than of one that in Britain is born.
I pray heaven so spacious,
To Britain be gracious,
Tho' some there be odious to both him and me;
Yet joy and renown,
And laurels shall crown
My *blackbird* with honour, wherever he be.

Tak your Auld Cloak about ye.

IN winter when the rain rain'd cauld,
    And froſt and ſnaw on ilka hill,
And Boreas, with his blaſts fae bald,
    Was threat'ning a' our ky to kill.
Then Bell, my wife, wha loves na ſtrife,
    She ſaid to me right haſtily,
Get up, goodman, ſave Cromie's life,
    And tak your auld cloak about ye.

My Cromie is an uſeful cow,
    And ſhe is come of a good kine;
Aft has ſhe wet the bairns' mou',
    And I am laith that ſhe ſhou'd tyne;
Get up, goodman, it is fou time,
    The ſun ſhines in the lift ſae hie;
Sloth never made a gracious end:
    Go tak your auld cloak about ye.

My cloak was anes a good grey cloak,
    When it was fitting for my wear;
But now it's ſcantly worth a groat,
    For I have worn't theſe thirty year:
Let's ſpend the gear that we have won,
    We little ken the day we'll die:
Then I'll be proud, ſince I have ſworn
    To have a new cloak about me.

In days when our King Robert rang,
    His trews they coſt but ha'f a crown;
He ſaid, they were a groat o'er dear,
    And call'd the taylor thief and loun.
He was the king that wore the crown,
    And thou'rt a man of laigh degree;
'Tis pride puts a' the country down,
    Sae tak thy auld cloak about thee.

Every land has its ain laugh,
　　Ilk kind of corn it has its hool;
I think the warld is a' run wrang,
　　When ilka wife her man wad rule.
Do ye not fee Rob, Jock, and Hab,
　　As they are girded gallantly,
While I fit hurklen in the afe?
　　I'll have a new cloak about me.

Goodman, I wat it's thirty years
　　Since we did ane anither ken;
And we have had between us twa,
　　Of lads and bonny laffes ten:
Now they are women grown and men,
　　I wifh and pray well may they be;
And if you prove a good hufband,
　　E'en tak yer auld cloak about ye.

Bell, my wife, fhe loves na ftrife;
　　But fhe wad guide me, if fhe can,
And to maintain an eafy life,
　　I aft maun yield, though I'm goodman:
Nought's to be won at woman's hand,
　　Unlefs ye give her a' the plea:
Then I'll leave aff where I began,
　　And tak my auld cloak about me.

The Quadruple Alliance.

Tune—Jocky blyth and gay.

SWIFT, SANDY, YOUNG, and GAY,
　　Are ftill my heart's delight,
I fing their fangs by day,
　　And read their tales at night.

If frae their books I be,
'Tis dulnefs then with me;
But when thefe ftars appear,
Jokes, fmiles, and wit fhine clear.

Swift, with uncommon ftyle,
  And wit that flows with eafe,
Inftructs us with a fmile,
  And never fails to pleafe.
    Bright Sandy gladly fings,
    Of heroes, gods, and kings:
    He well deferves the bays,
    And every Briton's praife.

While thus our Homer fhines,
  Young, with Horatian flame,
Corrects thefe falfe defigns
  We pufh in love of fame.
    Blyth Gay, in pawky ftrains,
    Makes villains, clowns, and fwains
    Reprove, with biting leer,
    Thofe in a higher fphere.

Swift, Sandy, Young, and Gay,
  Long may you give delight;
Let all the *dunces* bray,
  You're far above their fpite:
    Such, from a malice four,
    Write nonfenfe, lame and poor,
    Which never can fucceed,
    For who the trafh will read?

The end of the FIRST VOLUME.

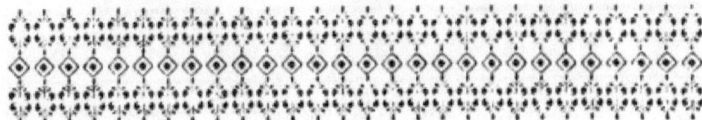

A COLLECTION
OF
CHOICE SONGS

*She sung—the youth attention gave,
And charms on charms espies:
Then all in raptures falls a slave,
Both to her voice and eyes.*

VOLUME II.

To Clarinda.
A SONG.

Tune—*I wish my love were in a mire.*

BLESS'D as th' immortal gods is he,
　　The youth who fondly sits by thee,
And hears and sees thee all the while
Softly speak, and sweetly smile, &c.
So spoke and smil'd the eastern maid;
　　Like thine, seraphic were her charms,
That in Circasia's vineyards stray'd,
　　And bless'd the wisest monarch's arms.

A thousand fair of high desert,
　　Strave to enchant the amorous king;
But the Circasian gain'd his heart,
　　And taught the royal bard to sing.

Clarinda thus our fang infpires,
　　And claims the fmooth and higheft lays,
But while each charm our bofom fires,
　　Words feem too few to found her praife.

Her mind in ev'ry grace complete,
　　To paint furpaffes human fkill :
Her majefty, mix'd with the fweet,
　　Let feraphs fing her if they will.
Whilft wond'ring with a ravifh'd eye,
　　We all that's perfect in her view,
Viewing a fifter of the fky,
　　To whom an adoration's due.

SONG.

Tune—*Lochaber no more.*

FAREWELL to Lochaber, and farewell my Jean,
　　Where heartfome with thee I've mony day been;
For Lochaber no more, Lochaber no more,
We'll may be return to Lochaber no more.
Thefe tears that I fhed, they are a' for my dear,
And no for the dangers attending on weir,
Tho' bore on rough feas to a far bloody fhore,
May be to return to Lochaber no more.

　Tho' hurricanes rife, and rife ev'ry wind,
They'll ne'er make a tempeft like that in my mind.
Tho' loudeft of thunder on louder waves roar,
That's naething like leaving my love on the fhore.
To leave thee behind me my heart is fair pain'd,
By eafe that's inglorious, no fame can be gain'd.
And beauty and love's the reward of the brave,
And I muft deferve it before I can crave.

Then glory, my Jeany, maun plead my excufe,
Since honour commands me, how can I refufe?
Without it I ne'er can have merit for thee,
And without thy favour I'd better not be.
I gae then, my lafs, to win honour and fame,
And if I fhould luck to come glorioufly hame,
I'll bring a heart to thee with love running o'er,
And then I'll leave thee and Lochaber no more.

The auld Goodman.

LATE in an evening forth I went,
   A little before the fun gae'd down,
And there I chanc'd by accident,
   To light on a battle new begun.
A man and his wife was fa'n in a ftrife,
   I canna well tell you how it began;
But ay fhe wail'd her wretched life,
   And cry'd ever, Alake, my auld goodman.

HE.

Thy auld goodman that thou tells of,
   The country kens where he was born,
Was but a filly poor vagabond,
   And ilka ane leugh him to fcorn;
For he did fpend, and make an end
   Of gear that his forefathers wan,
He gart the poor ftand frae the door,
   Sae tell nae mair of thy auld goodman.

SHE.

My heart, alake, is liken to break,
   When I think on my winfome John,
His blinkin eye, and gate fae free,
   Was naething like thee, thou dofen'd drone.

His rosie face, and flaxen hair,
   And a skin as white as ony swan,
Was large and tall, and comely withal,
   And thou'lt never be like my auld goodman.

HE.

Why dost thou pleen? I thee maintain,
   For meal and mawt thou disna want;
But thy wild bees I canna please,
   Now when our gear 'gins to grow scant.
Of houshold stuff thou hast enough,
   Thou wants for neither pot nor pan;
Of siklike ware he left thee bare,
   Sae tell nae mair of thy auld goodman.

SHE.

Yes, I may tell, and fret mysell,
   To think on these blyth days I had,
When he and I together lay
   In arms into a well-made bed;
But now I sigh and may be sad,
   Thy courage is cauld, thy colour wan,
Thou falds thy feet, and fa's asleep,
   And thou'lt ne'er be like my auld goodman.

Then coming was the night sae dark,
   And gane was a' the light o' day;
The carl was fear'd to miss his mark,
   And therefore wad nae langer stay;
Then up he gat, and he ran his way,
   I trow the wife the day she wan,
And ay the o'erword of the fray
   Was ever, *Alake, my auld goodman.*   Z.

SONG.

Tune—*Valiant* JOCKY.

On a beautiful, but very young lady.

BEAUTY from fancy takes its arms,
   And ev'ry common face fome breaſt may move.
Some in a look, a ſhape, or air find charms,
   To juſtify their choice, or boaſt their love.
But had the great Apelles feen that face,
   When he the Cyprian goddeſs drew,
He had neglected all the female race,
   Thrown his firſt Venus by, and copied you.
     In that deſign,
     Great nature would combine
   To fix the ſtandard of her ſacred coin;
   The charming figure had enhanc'd his fame,
   And ſhrines been rais'd to Seraphina's name.

II.

But fince no painter ere could take
   That face which baffles all his curious art;
And he that ſtrives the bold attempt to make,
   As well might paint the fecrets of the heart.
O happy glaſs, I'll thee prefer,
   Content to be, like thee, inanimate,
Since only to be gaz'd on thus by her,
   A better life and motion would create.
     Her eyes would inſpire,
     And like Prometheus's fire,
   At once inform the piece and give defire;
   The charming phantom I would graſp, and fly
   O'er all the orb, though in that moment die.

III.

Let meaner beauties fear the day,
   Whoſe charms are fading, and fubmit to time;
The graces which from them it ſteals away,
   It with a laviſh hand ſtill adds to thine.

The god of love in ambush lies,
  And with his arms surrounds the fair,
He points his conquering arrows in these eyes,
  Then hangs a sharpen'd dart at ev'ry hair,
    As with fatal skill,
    Turn which way you will,
    Like Eden's flaming-sword each way you kill;
So rip'ning years improve rich nature's store,
And gives perfection to the golden ore.   P.

Lass with a Lump of Land.

GI'E me a lass with a lump of land,
  And we for life shall gang the gither,
Though daft or wise, I'll never demand,
  Or black or fair, it maksna whether.
I'm aff with wit, and beauty will fade,
  And bloom alane is na worth a shilling;
But she that's rich, her market's made,
  For ilka charm about her is killing.

Gi'e me a lass with a lump of land,
  And in my bosom I'll hug my treasure;
Gin I had anes her gear in my hand,
  Should love turn douf, it will find pleasure.
Laugh on wha likes, but there's my hand,
  I hate with poortith, though bonny, to meddle,
Unless they bring cash, or a lump of land,
  Theyse never get me to dance to their fiddle.

There's meikle good love in bands and bags,
  And siller and gowd's a sweet complexion;
But beauty, and wit, and virtue in rags,
  Have tint the art of gaining affection:
Love tips his arrows with woods and parks,
  And castles, and riggs, and muirs, and meadows,
And naithing can catch our modern sparks,
  But well-tocher'd lasses, or jointur'd widows.

The Shepherd Adonis.

I.

THE shepherd Adonis
　　Being weary'd with sport,
He, for a retirement,
　　To the woods did resort;
He threw by his club,
　　And he laid himself down;
He envy'd no monarch,
　　Nor wish'd for a crown.

II.

He drank of the burn,
　　And he ate frae the tree,
Himself he enjoy'd,
　　And frae trouble was free.
He wish'd for no nymph,
　　Though never sae fair,
Had nae love nor ambition,
　　And therefore no care.

III.

But as he lay thus
　　In an ev'ning sae clear,
A heavn'ly sweet voice
　　Sounded saft in his ear;
Which came frae a shady
　　Green neighbouring grove,
Where bonny Amynta
　　Sat singing of love.

IV.

He wander'd that way,
　　And found wha was there,
He was quite confounded
　　To see her sae fair:

He stood like a statue,
    Not a foot cou'd he move,
Nor knew he what griev'd him;
    But he fear'd it was love.

V.

The nymph she beheld him
    With a kind modest grace,
Seeing something that pleas'd her
    Appear in his face,
With blushing a little
    She to him did say,
Oh shepherd! what want ye,
    How came you this way?

VI.

His spirits reviving,
    He to her reply'd,
I was ne'er sae surpris'd
    At the sight of a maid;
Until I beheld thee,
    From love I was free;
But now I'm ta'en captive,
    My fairest, by thee.   Z.

The Complaint.

To B. I. G.

Tune—*When absent,* &c.

WHEN absent from the nymph I love,
    I'd fain shake off the chains I wear;
But whilst I strive these to remove,
    More fetters I'm oblig'd to bear.

My captiv'd fancy day and night
　　Fairer and fairer reprefents
Belinda form'd for dear delight,
　　But cruel caufe of my complaints.

All day I wander through the groves,
　　And fighing hear from ev'ry tree
The happy birds chirping their loves,
　　Happy, compar'd with lonely me.
When gentle fleep with balmy wings
　　To reft fans ev'ry weary'd wight,
A thoufand fears my fancy brings,
　　That keep me watching all the night.

Sleep flies, while like the goddefs fair,
　　And all the graces in her train,
With melting fmiles and killing air
　　Appears the caufe of all my pain.
A while my mind delighted flies
　　O'er all her fweets with thirling joy,
Whilft want of worth makes doubts arife,
　　That all my trembling hopes deftroy.

Thus while my thoughts are fixed on her,
　　I'm all o'er tranfport and defire;
My pulfe beats high, my cheek appears
　　All rofes, and mine eyes all fire.
When to myfelf I turn my view,
　　My veins grow chill, my cheeks look wan:
Thus whilft my fears my pains renew,
　　I fcarcely look or move a man.

The young Lafs *contra* auld Man.

THE carl he came o'er the croft,
　　And his beard new fhav'n,
He look'd at me, as he'd been daft,
　　The carl trows that I wad hae him.

Howt awa, I winna hae him!
   Na, forfooth, I winna hae him!
For a' his beard new fhav'n,
   Ne'er a bit will I hae him.

A filler broach he gae me neift,
   To faften on my curchea nooked,
I wor'd a wee upon my breaft,
   But foon, alake! the tongue o't crooked;
And fae may his, I winna hae him!
   Na, forfooth, I winna hae him!
Ane twice a bairn's a lafs's jeft;
   Sae ony fool for me may hae him.

The carl has na fault but ane;
   For he has land and dollars plenty;
But waes me for him! fkin and bane
   Is no for a plump lafs of twenty.
Howt awa, I winna hae him!
   Na, forfooth, I winna hae him!
What fignifies his dirty riggs,
   And cafh, without a man with them

But fhou'd my cankard daddy gar
   Me tak him 'gainft my inclination,
I warn the fumbler to beware,
   That antlers dinna claim their ftation.
Howt awa, I winna hae him!
   Na, forfooth, I winna hae him!
I'm fleed to crack the haly band,
   Sae lawty fays, I fhou'd na hae him.

VIRTUE and WIT.
The Prefervatives of Love and Beauty.
Tune—*Killikranky.*

HE.

CONFESS thy love, fair blufhing maid,
    For fince thine eye's confenting,
Thy fafter thoughts are a' betray'd,
    And na-fays no worth tenting.
Why aims thou to oppofe thy mind,
    With words thy wifh denying?
Since nature made thee to be kind,
    Reafon allows complying.

Nature and reafon's joint confent
    Make love a facred bleffing,
Then happily that time is fpent,
    That's war'd on kind careffing.
Come then, my Katie, to my arms,
    I'll be nae mair a rover;
But find out heav'n in a' thy charms,
    And prove a faithful lover.

SHE.

What you defign, by nature's law,
    Is fleeting inclination,
That Willy-Wifp bewilds us a'
    By its infatuation.
When that goes out, careffes tire,
    And love's na mair in feafon,
Syne weakly we blow up the fire,
    With all our boafted reafon.

HE.

The beauties of inferior caft
    May ftart this juft reflection;
But charms like thine maun always laft,
    Where wit has the protection.

Virtue and Wit, like April rays,
　　Make beauty rife the sweeter;
The langer then on thee I gaze,
　　My love will grow completer.

SONG.

Tune—*The happy clown.*

IT was the charming month of May,
　　When all the flow'rs were fresh and gay,
One morning by the break of day,
　　　　Sweet Chloe, chaste and fair;
From peaceful slumber she arose,
Girt on her mantle and her hose,
And o'er the flow'ry mead she goes,
　　　　To breathe a purer air.

　　Her looks so sweet, so gay her mien,
Her handsome shape, and dress so clean,
She look'd all o'er like beauty's queen,
　　　　Drest in her best array.
The gentle winds, and purling stream,
Assay'd to whisper Chloe's name,
The savage beasts, till then ne'er tame,
　　　　Wild adoration pay.

　　The feather'd people, one might see,
Perch'd all around her on a tree;
With notes of sweetest melody
　　　　They act a chearful part.
The dull slaves on the toilsome plow,
Their wearied necks and knees do bow,
A glad subjection there they vow,
　　　　To pay with all their heart.

The bleating flocks that then came by,
Soon as the charming nymph they fpy,
They leave their hoarfe and rueful cry,
   And dance around the brooks.
The woods are glad, the meadows fmile,
And Forth, that foam'd and roar'd erewhile,
Glides calmly down and fmooth as oil,
   Thro' all its charming crooks.

The finny fquadrons are content
To leave their wat'ry element,
In glazie numbers down they bent,
   They flutter all along.
The infects and each creeping thing,
Join'd to make up the rural ring;
All frifk and dance, if fhe but fing,
   And make a jovial throng.

Kind Phœbus now began to rife,
And paint with red the eaftern fkies,
Struck with the glory of her eyes,
   He fhrinks behind a cloud.
Her mantle on a bow fhe lays,
And all her glory fhe difplays,
She left all nature in amaze,
   And fkipp'd into the wood.   X.

Lady ANNE BOTHWELL'S Lament.

BALOW, my boy, lie ftill and fleep,
 It grieves me fore to hear thee weep:
If thou'lt be filent, I'll be glad,
Thy mourning makes my heart full fad.
Balow, my boy, thy mother's joy,
Thy father bred me great annoy.
 Balow, my boy, lie ftill and fleep,
 It grieves me fore to hear thee weep.

Balow, my darling, sleep a while,
And when thou wak'st, then sweetly smile;
But smile not as thy father did,
To cozen maids; nay, God forbid;
For in thine eye his look I see,
The tempting look that ruin'd me.
  Balow, my boy, &c.

When he began to court my love,
And with his sugar'd words to move,
His tempting face, and flatt'ring chear,
In time to me did not appear;
But now I see that cruel he
Cares neither for his babe nor me.
  Balow, my boy, &c.

Farewel, farewel, thou falsest youth
That ever kiss'd a woman's mouth;
Let never any after me
Submit unto thy courtesy:
For, if they do, O! cruel thou
Wilt her abuse, and care not how.
  Balow, my boy, &c.

I was too cred'lous at the first,
To yield thee all a maiden durst;
Thou swore for ever true to prove,
Thy faith unchang'd, unchang'd thy love;
But quick as thought the change is wrought,
Thy love's no more, thy promise nought.
  Balow, my boy, &c.

I wish I were a maid again,
From young men's flattery I'd refrain;
For now, unto my grief, I find,
They all are perjur'd and unkind:
Bewitching charms bred all my harms,
Witness my babe lies in my arms.
  Balow, my boy, &c.

I take my fate from bad to worfe,
That I muft needs be now a nurfe,
And lull my young fon on my lap;
From me, fweet orphan, take the pap.
Balow, my child, thy mother mild
Shall wail, as from all blifs exil'd.
  Balow, my boy, &c.

Balow, my boy, weep not for me,
Whofe greateft grief's for wronging thee,
Nor pity her deferved fmart,
Who can blame none but her fond heart;
For too foon trufting lateft finds,
With faireft tongues are falfeft minds.
  Balow, my boy, &c.

Balow, my boy, thy father's fled,
When he the thriftlefs fon has play'd;
Of vows and oaths forgetful, he
Preferr'd the wars to thee and me.
But now, perhaps, thy curfe and mine
Make him eat acorns with the fwine.
  Balow, my boy, &c.

But curfe not him; perhaps now he,
Stung with remorfe, is blefling thee:
Perhaps at death; for who can tell
Whether the judge of heaven or hell,
By fome proud foe has ftruck the blow,
And laid the dear deceiver low.
  Balow, my boy, &c.

I wifh I were into the bounds
Where he lies fmother'd in his wounds,
Repeating, as he pants for air,
My name, whom once he call'd his fair.
No woman's yet fo fiercely fet,
But fhe'll forgive, though not forget.
  Balow, my boy, &c.

If linen lacks, for my love's fake,
Then quickly to him would I make
My fmock once for his body meet,
And wrap him in that winding-fheet.
Ah me! how happy had I been,
If he had ne'er been wrapt therein.
 Balow, my boy, &c.

Balow, my boy, I'll weep for thee;
Too foon, alake, thou'lt weep for me:
Thy griefs are growing to a fum,
God grant thee patience when they come;
Born to fuftain thy mother's fhame,
A haplefs fate, a baftard's name.
 Balow, my boy, lie ftill and fleep,
 It grieves me fore to hear thee weep. X.

SONG.
She raife and loot me in.

THE night her filent fable wore,
 And gloomy were the fkies;
Of glitt'ring ftars appear'd no more
 Than thofe in Nelly's eyes.
When at her father's yate I knock'd,
 Where I had often been,
She, fhrouded only with her fmock,
 Arofe and loot me in.

Faft lock'd within her clofe embrace,
 She trembling ftood afham'd;
Her fwelling breaft, and glowing face,
 And ev'ry touch inflam'd.
My eager paffion I obey'd,
 Refolv'd the fort to win;
And her fond heart was foon betray'd
 To yield and let me in.

Then, then, beyond expreſſing,
  Tranſporting was the joy;
I knew no greater bleſſing,
  So bleſs'd a man was I.
And ſhe, all raviſh'd with delight,
  Bid me oft come again;
And kindly vow'd, that ev'ry night
  She'd riſe and let me in.

But ah! at laſt ſhe prov'd with bairn,
  And ſighing ſat and dull,
And I that was as much concern'd,
  Look'd e'en juſt like a fool.
Her lovely eyes with tears ran o'er,
  Repenting her raſh ſin:
She ſigh'd, and curſt the fatal hour
  That e'er ſhe loot me in.

But who cou'd cruelly deceive,
  Or from ſuch beauty part?
I lov'd her ſo, I could not leave
  The charmer of my heart;
But wedded, and conceal'd our crime:
  Thus all was well again,
And now ſhe thanks the happy time
  That e'er ſhe loot me in.   Z.

SONG.

If love's a ſweet paſſion.

IF love's a ſweet paſſion, why does it torment?
  If a bitter, O tell me whence comes my complaint?
Since I ſuffer with pleaſure, why ſhould I complain,
Or grieve at my fate, ſince I know 'tis in vain?
Yet ſo pleaſing the pain is, ſo ſoft is the dart,
That at once it both wounds me, and tickles my heart.

K

I grasp her hands gently, look languishing down,
And, by passionate silence, I make my love known:
But oh! how I'm bless'd when so kind she does prove,
By some willing mistake to discover her love;
When in striving to hide, she reveals all her flame,
And our eyes tell each other what neither dare name.

How pleasing is beauty! how sweet are the charms!
How delightful embraces! how peaceful her arms!
Sure there is nothing so easy as learning to love;
'Tis taught us on earth, and by all things above:
And to beauty's bright standard all heroes must yield,
For 'tis beauty that conquers, and wins the fair field.

X.

John Ochiltree.

HONEST man, John Ochiltree;
  Mine ain auld John Ochiltree,
Wilt thou come o'er the moor to me,
And dance as thou was wont to do?
Alake, alake! I wont to do!
Ohon, ohon! I wont to do!
Now wont to do's away frae me,
Frae silly auld John Ochiltree.
Honest man, John Ochiltree;
Mine ain auld John Ochiltree:
Come anes out o'er the moor to me,
And do but what thou dow to do.
Alake, alake! I dow to do!
Walaways! I dow to do!
To whost and hirple o'er my tree,
My bonny moor-powt, is a' I may do.

Walaways! John Ochiltree,
For mony a time I tell'd to thee,

Thou rade fae faft by fea and land,
And wadna keep a bridle hand,
Thou'd tine the beaft, thy fell wad die,
My filly auld John Ochiltree.
Come to my arms, my bonny thing,
And chear me up to hear thee fing;
And tell me o'er a' we hae done,
For thoughts maun now my life fuftain.

Gae thy ways, John Ochiltree:
Hae done! it has nae fa'r wi' me,
I'll fet the beaft in throw the land.
She'll maybe fa' in a better hand,
Even fit thou there and drink thy fill,
For I'll do as I wont to do ftill.   Z.

SONG.

Tune—*Jenny beguil'd the webfter.*

The auld chorus.

Up ftairs, down ftairs,
  Timber ftairs fear me,
I'm laith to ly a night my lane,
  And Johny's bed's fae near me.

O Mither dear, I 'gin to fear,
    Though I'm baith good and bonny,
I winna keep; for in my fleep
    I ftart, and dream of Johny.
When Johny then comes down the glen
    To woo me, dinna hinder;
But with content gi'e your confent,
    For we twa ne'er can finder.

Better to marry, than mifcarry;
  For fhame and fkaith's the clink o't;
To thole the dool, to mount the ftool,
  I downa bide to think o't;
Sae while it's time, I'll fhun the crime
  That gars poor Epps gae whinging,
With haunches fow, and een fae blew,
  To a' the bedrals binging.

Had Eppy's apron bidden down,
  The Kirk had ne'er a ken'd it;
But when the word's gane thro' the town,
  Alake, how can fhe mend it?
Now Tam maun face the minifter,
  And fhe maun mount the pillar:
And that's the way that they maun gae,
  For poor folk has nae filler.

Now had ye'r tongue, my daughter young,
  Replied the kindly mither,
Get Johny's hand, in haly band,
  Syne wap your wealth togither.
I'm o' the mind, if he be kind,
  Ye'll do your part difcreetly;
And prove a wife will gar his life
  And barrel run right fweetly.

++

SONG.

Tune—*Wat ye wha I met yeftreen*, &c.

OF all the birds whofe tuneful throats
  Do welcome in the verdant fpring,
I far prefer the Stirling's notes,
  And think fhe does moft fweetly fing.

Nor thrush, nor linnet, nor the bird
  Brought from the far Canary coast,
Nor can the nightingale afford,
  Such melody as she can boast.

When Phœbus southward darts his fires,
  And on our plains he looks askance,
The nightingale with him retires,
  My Stirling makes my blood to dance.
In spite of Hyems' nipping frost,
  Whether the day be dark or clear,
Shall I not to her health entoast,
  Who makes it summer all the year?

Then by thyself, my lovely bird,
  I'll stroke thy back, and kiss thy breast;
And if you'll take my honest word,
  As sacred as before the priest,
I'll bring thee where I will devise
  Such various ways to pleasure thee,
The velvet fog thou wilt despise,
  When on the *downy hills with me*.   T. R.

SONG.

To its own Tune.

IN January last,
  On Munanday at morn,
As thro' the fields I past,
  To view the winter corn,
I looked me behind,
  And saw come o'er the know,
And glancing in her apron,
  With a bonny brent brow.

I faid, Good-morrow, fair maid;
  And fhe right court'oufly
Return'd a beck, and kindly faid,
  Good-day, sweet Sir, to you.
I fpear'd, My dear, how far awa
  Do ye intend to gae?
Quoth fhe, I mean a mile or twa
  Out o'er yon broomy brae.

HE.

Fair maid, I'm thankfu' to my fate,
  To have fic company;
For I am ganging ftraight that gate,
  Where ye intend to be.
When we had gane a mile or twain,
  I faid to her, My dow,
May we not lean us on this plain,
  And kifs your bonny mou'?

SHE.

Kind Sir, ye are a wee miftane;
  For I am nane of thefe,
I hope ye fome mair breeding ken,
  Than to ruffle women's claife:
For may be I have chofen ane,
  And plighted him my vow,
Wha may do wi' me what he likes,
  And kifs my bonny mou'.

HE.

Na, if ye are contracted,
  I hae na mair to fay:
Rather than be rejected,
  I will gi'e o'er the play;
And chufe anither will refpect
  My love and on me rew;
And let me clafp her round the neck,
  And kifs her bonny mou'.

SHE.

O Sir, ye are proud-hearted,
　And laith to be faid nay,
Elfe ye wad ne'er a ſtarted
　For ought that I did fay:
For women in their modeſty,
　At firſt they winna bow;
But if we like your company,
　We'll prove as kind as you.　　Z.

SONG.

Tune—I'll never leave thee.

ONE day I heard Mary fay,
　How fhall I leave thee?
Stay, deareſt Adonis, ſtay,
　Why wilt thou grieve me?
Alas! my fond heart will break,
　If thou ſhould leave me.
I'll live and die for thy fake:
　Yet never leave thee.

Say, lovely Adonis, fay,
　Has Mary deceiv'd thee?
Did e'er her young heart betray
　New love, that has griev'd thee?
My conſtant mind ne'er ſhall ſtray,
　Thou may believe me.
I'll love thee, lad, night and day,
　And never leave thee.

Adonis, my charming youth,
　What can relieve thee?
Can Mary thy anguiſh footh!
　This breaſt ſhall receive thee.

My paſſion can ne'er decay,
  Never deceive thee:
Delight ſhall drive pain away,
  Pleaſure revive thee.

But leave thee, leave thee, lad,
  How ſhall I leave thee?
O! that thought makes me ſad,
  I'll never leave thee.
Where would my Adonis fly?
  Why does he grieve me?
Alas! my poor heart will die,
  If I ſhould leave thee.   C.

Sleepy Body, drowſy Body.

SOMNOLENTE, quæſo, repente
  Vigila, vive, me tange.
Somnolente, quæſo, repente
Vigila, vive, me tange.
  Cum me ambiebas,
  Videri ſolebas
Amoris negotiis aptus;
  At factus maritus,
  In lecto ſopitus,
Somno es, haud amore, tu captus.

  O ſleepy body,
  And drowſy body,
O wiltuna waken, and turn thee:
  To drivel and draunt,
  While I ſigh and gaunt,
Gives me good reaſon to ſcorn thee.

When thou fhouldft be kind,
Thou turns fleepy and blind,
And fnoters and fnores far frae me.
Wae light on thy face,
Thy drowfy embrace
Is enough to gar me betray thee.   Q.

General Lesly's March to Longmarfton Moor.

MARCH, march,
  Why the d—— do ye na march?
Stand to your arms, my lads,
  Fight in good order,
Front about, ye mufketeers all,
  Till ye come to the Englifh border:
    Stand till't, and fight like men,
    True gofpel to maintain,
The parliament's blyth to fee us a' coming.
    When to the kirk we come,
    We'll purge it ilka room,
Frae Popifh relics, and a' fic innovations,
    That a' the warld may fee,
    There's nane i' the right but we,
Of the auld Scottifh nation.
Jenny fhall wear the hood,
Jocky the fark of God;
And the kift fou of whiftles,
That make fic a cleiro,
    Our pipers braw,
    Shall hae them a',
    Whate'er come on it,
    Bufk up your plaids, my lads,
    Cock up your bonnets.
March, march, &c.   Z.

SONG.

Tune—I'll gar ye be fain to follow me.

HE.

ADIEU, for a while, my native green plains,
My neareſt relations, and neighbouring ſwains,
Dear Nelly, frae theſe I'd ſtart eaſily free,
Were minutes not ages, while abſent frae thee.

SHE.

Then tell me the reaſon thou does not obey
The pleadings of love, but thus hurries away;
Alake, thou deceiver, o'er plainly I ſee,
A lover ſae roving will never mind me.

HE.

The reaſon unhappy, is owing to fate
That gave me a being without an eſtate,
Which lays a neceſſity now upon me,
To purchaſe a fortune for pleaſure to thee.

SHE.

Small fortune may ſerve where love has the ſway,
Then, Johny, be counſell'd na langer to ſtray;
For while thou proves conſtant in kindneſs to me,
Contented I'll ay find a treaſure in thee.

HE.

O ceaſe, my dear charmer, elſe ſoon I'll betray
A weakneſs unmanly, and quickly give way
To fondneſs which may prove a ruin to thee,
A pain to us baith, and diſhonour to me.

Bear witneſs, ye ſtreams, and witneſs, ye flowers:
Bear witneſs, ye watchful inviſible powers,
If ever my heart be unfaithful to thee,
May naithing propitious e'er ſmile upon me.

SONG.

To the tune of

BUSK ye, buſk ye, my bonny bride;
  Buſk ye, buſk ye, my bonny marrow;
Buſk ye, buſk ye, my bonny bride,
  Buſk and go to the braes of Yarrow;
There will we ſport and gather dew,
  Dancing while laverocks ſing the morning;
There learn frae turtles to prove true;
  O Bell! ne'er vex me with thy ſcorning.

To weſtlin breezes Flora yields,
  And when the beams are kindly warming,
Blythneſs appears o'er all the fields,
  And nature looks mair freſh and charming.
Learn frae the burns that trace the mead,
  Tho' on their banks the roſes bloſſom,
Yet haſtilie they flow to Tweed,
  And pour their ſweetneſs in his boſom.

Haſte ye, haſte ye, my bonny Bell,
  Haſte to my arms, and there I'll guard thee,
With free conſent my fears repel,
  I'll with my love and care reward thee.
Thus ſang I ſaftly to my fair,
  Who rais'd my hopes with kind relenting.
O queen of ſmiles, I aſk na mair,
  Since now my bonny Bell's conſenting.

Corn-riggs are bonny.

MY Patie is a lover gay,
  His mind is never muddy,
His breath is ſweeter than new hay,
  His face is fair and ruddy.

His shape is handsome, middle size;
　　He's stately in his wawking;
The shining of his een surprise;
　　'Tis heaven to hear him tawking.

Last night I met him on a bawk,
　　Where yellow corn was growing,
There mony a kindly word he spake,
　　That set my heart a-glowing.
He kiss'd, and vow'd he wad be mine,
　　And loo'd me best of ony;
That gars me like to sing sinsyne,
　　O corn-riggs are bonny.

Let maidens of a silly mind
　　Refuse what maist they're wanting,
Since we for yielding are design'd,
　　We chastly should be granting;
Then I'll comply and marry Pate,
　　And syne my cockernony
He's free to touzle air or late,
　　Where corn-riggs are bonny.

Cromlet's Lilt.

SINCE all thy vows, false maid,
　　Are blown to air,
And my poor heart betray'd
　　To sad despair,
Into some wilderness,
My grief I will express,
And thy hard-heartedness,
　　O cruel air.

Have I not graven our loves
　　On every tree,
In yonder spreading groves,
　　Tho' false thou be?

Was not a solemn oath
Plighted betwixt us both,
Thou thy faith, I my troth,
    Constant to be?

Some gloomy place I'll find,
    Some doleful shade,
Where neither sun nor wind
    E'er entrance had:
Into that hollow cave,
There will I sigh and rave,
Because thou dost behave
    So faithlessly.

Wild-fruit shall be my meat,
    I'll drink the spring,
Cold earth shall be my seat:
    For covering
I'll have the starry sky
My head to canopy,
Until my soul on hy
    Shall spread its wing.

I'll have no funeral fire,
    Nor tears for me:
No grave do I desire,
    Nor obsequies:
The courteous Red-breast he
With leaves will cover me,
And sing my elegy
    With doleful voice.

And when a ghost I am,
    I'll visit thee,
O thou deceitful dame,
    Whose cruelty
Has kill'd the kindest heart
That e'er felt Cupid's dart,
And never can desert
    From loving thee.   X.

SONG.

We'll a' to Kelso go.

AN I'll awa to bonny Tweedſide,
  And fee my deary come throw,
And he fall be mine,
Gif fae he incline,
For I hate to lead *apes* below.

While young and fair
  I'll make it my care,
To fecure myſelf in a jo;
  I'm no ſic a fool
  To let my blood cool,
And fyne gae lead *apes* below.

Few words, bonny lad,
  Will eithly perfuade,
Tho' bluſhing, I daftly fay, no,
  Gae on with your ſtrain,
  And doubt not to gain,
For I hate to lead *apes* below.

Unty'd to a man,
  Do what'er we can,
We never can thrive or dow:
  Then I will do well,
  Do better what will,
And let them lead *apes* below.

Our time is precious,
  And gods are gracious
That beauties upon us beſtow;
  'Tis not to be thought
  We got them for nought,
Or to be ſet up for a ſhow.

'Tis carried by votes,
  Come kilt up your coats,
And let us to Edinburgh go,
  Where fhe that's bonny
  May catch a Johny,
And never lead *apes* below.

WILLIAM and MARGARET.

An old ballad.

'TWAS at the fearful midnight hour,
  When all were faſt aſleep,
In glided Margaret's grimly ghoſt,
  And ſtood at William's feet.

Her face was pale like April morn;
  Clad in a wintry cloud;
And clay-cold was her lily-hand
  That held her fable ſhroud.

So ſhall the faireſt face appear,
  When youth and years are flown;
Such is the robe that kings muſt wear,
  When death has reft their crown.

Her bloom was like the ſpringing flow'r,
  That ſips the ſilver dew;
The roſe was budded in her cheek,
  Juſt op'ning to the view.

But love had, like the canker-worm,
  Confum'd her early prime:
The roſe grew pale, and left her cheek;
  She dy'd before her time.

Awake!—fhe cry'd, thy true love calls,
    Come from her midnight grave:
Now let thy pity hear the maid
    Thy love refus'd to fave.

This is the dumb and dreary hour,
    When injur'd ghofts complain,
And aid the fecret fears of night,
    To fright the faithlefs man.

Bethink thee, William, of thy fault,
    Thy pledge and broken oath,
And give me back my maiden-vow,
    And give me back my troth.

How could you fay my face was fair,
    And yet that face forfake?
How could you win that virgin-heart,
    Yet leave that heart to break?

Why did you promife love to me,
    And not that promife keep?
Why faid you, that my eyes were bright,
    Yet left thefe eyes to weep?

How could you fwear my lip was fweet,
    And made the fcarlet pale?
And why did I, young witlefs maid,
    Believe the flatt'ring tale?

That face, alas! no more is fair;
    Thefe lips no longer red;
Dark are my eyes, now clos'd in death,
    And ev'ry charm is fled.

The hungry worm my fifter is;
    This winding-fheet I wear:
And cold and weary lafts our night,
    Till that laft morn appear.

But hark!—the cock has warn'd me hence—
　　A long and late adieu!
Come fee, falfe man, how low fhe lies
　　That dy'd for love of you.

The lark fung out, the morning fmil'd,
　　And rais'd her glifl'ring head;
Pale William quak'd in ev'ry limb;
　　Then, raving, left his bed.

He hy'd him to the fatal place
　　Where Margaret's body lay,
And ftretch'd him o'er the green grafs turf
　　That wrapt her breathlefs clay.

And thrice he call'd on Margaret's name,
　　And thrice he wept full fore:
Then laid his cheek on her cold grave,
　　And word fpoke never more.　　D. M.

The Complaint.

THE fun was funk beneath the hill,
　　The weftern cloud was lin'd with gold:
Clear was the fky, the wind was ftill,
　　The flocks were penn'd within the fold:
When in the filence of the grove,
Poor Damon thus defpair'd of love.

Who feeks to pluck the fragrant rofe,
　　From the hard rock or oozy beach;
Who from each weed that barren grows,
　　Expects the grape or downy peach;
With equal faith may hope to find
The truth of love in womankind.

No flocks have I, or fleecy care,
  No fields that wave with golden grain,
No pastures green, or gardens fair,
  A woman's venal heart to gain.
Then all in vain my sighs must prove,
Whose whole estate, alas! is love.

How wretched is the faithful youth,
  Since women's hearts are bought and sold!
They ask no vows of sacred truth;
  Whene'er they sigh, they sigh to gold.
Gold can the frowns of scorn remove;—
Thus I am scorn'd,—who have but love.

To buy the gems of India's coast,
  What wealth, what riches would suffice?
Yet India's shore should never boast
  The lustre of thy rival eyes;
For there the world too cheap must prove;
Can I then buy—who have but love?

Then, Mary, since nor gems nor ore
  Can with thy brighter self compare,
Be just, as fair, and value more
  Than gems or ore, a heart sincere:
Let treasure meaner beauties prove;
Who pays thy worth, must pay in love. X.

SONG.

Tune—*Montrose's lines.*

I TOSS and tumble through the night,
  And with th' approaching day,
Thinking when darkness yields to light,
  I'll banish care away:

But when the glorious fun doth rife,
    And chear all nature round,
All thoughts of pleafure in me dies;
    My cares do ftill abound.

My tortur'd and uneafy mind
    Bereaves me of my reft;
My thoughts are to all pleafure blind,
    With care I'm ftill oppreft:
But had I her within my breaft,
    Who gives me fo much pain,
My raptur'd foul would be at reft,
    And fofteft joys regain.

I'd not envy the god of war,
    Blefs'd with fair Venus' charms,
Nor yet the thund'ring Jupiter
    In fair Alcmena's arms:
Paris, with Helen's beauty blefs'd,
    Wou'd be a jeft to me;
If of her charms I were poffefs'd,
    Thrice happier wou'd I be.

But fince the gods do not ordain
    Such happy fate for me,
I dare not 'gainft their will repine,
    Who rule my deftiny.
With fprightly wine I'll drown my care,
    And cherifh up my foul;
Whene'er I think on my loft fair,
    I'll drown her in the bowl.   I. H., *Jamaica.*

The Deceiver.

WITH tuneful pipe and hearty glee,
    Young Watty wan my heart;
A blyther lad ye cou'dna fee,
    All beauty without art.

        His winning tale
        Did soon prevail
To gain my fond belief;
        But soon the swain
        Gangs o'er the plain,
And leaves me full, and leaves me full,
        And leaves me full of grief.

Tho' Colin courts with tuneful sang,
        Yet few regard his mane :
The lasses a' round Watty thrang,
        While Colin's left alane :
        In Aberdeen
        Was never seen
A lad that gave sic pain.
        He daily wooes,
        And still pursues,
Till he does all, till he does all,
        Till he does all obtain.

But soon as he has gain'd the bliss,
        Away then does he run,
And hardly will afford a kiss
        To silly me undone :
        Bonny Katy,
        Maggy, Beatty,
Avoid the roving swain ;
        His wily tongue
        Be sure to shun,
Or you like me, or you like me,
        Like me will be undone.   Z.

Sweet Susan.

Tune—*Leader-haughs.*

I.

THE morn was fair, faft was the air,
    All nature's fweets were fpringing;
The buds did bow with filver dew,
    Ten thoufand birds were finging:
When on the bent, with blyth content,
    Young Jamie fang his marrow,
Nae bonnier lafs e'er trod the grafs,
    On Leader-haughs and Yarrow.

II.

How fweet her face, where ev'ry grace
    In heav'nly beauty's planted;
Her fmiling een, and comely mien
    That nae perfection wanted.
I'll never fret, nor ban my fate,
    But blefs my bonny marrow;
If her dear fmile my doubts beguile,
    My mind fhall ken nae forrow.

III.

Yet tho' fhe's fair, and has full fhare
    Of every charm inchanting,
Each good turns ill, and foon will kill
    Poor me, if love be wanting.
O bonny lafs! have but the grace
    To think, ere ye gae furder,
Your joys maun flit, if ye commit
    The crying fin of murder.

IV.

My wand'ring ghaift will ne'er get reft,
    And night and day affright ye;
But if ye're kind, with joyful mind,
    I'll ftudy to delight ye.

Our years around with love thus crown'd,
　　From all things joy ſhall borrow;
Thus none ſhall be more bleſs'd than we
　　On Leader-haughs and Yarrow.

v.

O ſweeteſt Sue! 'tis only you
　　Can make life worth my wiſhes,
If equal love your mind can move
　　To grant this beſt of bliſſes.
Thou art my ſun, and thy leaſt frown
　　Would blaſt me in the bloſſom:
But if thou ſhine, and make me thine,
　　I'll flouriſh in thy boſom.

Cowdon-Knows.

WHEN ſummer comes, the ſwains on Tweed
　　Sing their ſucceſsful loves,
Around the ewes and lambkins feed,
　　And muſic fills the groves.

But my lov'd ſong is then the broom
　　So fair on Cowdon-knows;
For ſure ſo ſweet, ſo ſoft a bloom
　　Elſewhere there never grows.

There Colin tun'd his oaten reed,
　　And won my yielding heart;
No ſhepherd e'er that dwelt on Tweed
　　Could play with half ſuch art.

He ſung of Tay, of Forth, and Clyde,
　　The hills and dales all round,
Of Leader-haughs, and Leader-ſide,
　　Oh! how I bleſs'd the ſound.

Yet more delightful is the broom
  So fair on Cowdon-knows;
For sure so fresh, so bright a bloom
  Elsewhere there never grows.

Not Teviot braes so green and gay
  May with this broom compare,
Not Yarrow banks in flow'ry May,
  Nor the bush aboon Traquair.

More pleasing far are Cowdon-knows,
  My peaceful happy home,
Where I was wont to milk my ewes
  At even among the broom.

Ye powers that haunt the woods and plains
  Where Tweed with Teviot flows,
Convey me to the best of swains,
  And my lov'd Cowdon-knows.   C.

Sandy and Betty.

SANDY in Edinburgh was born,
  As blyth a lad as e'er gade thence:
Betty did Staffordshire adorn
  With all that's lovely to the sense.

Had Sandy still remain'd at hame,
  He had not blinkt on Betty's smile;
For why, he caught the gentle flame
  On this side Tweed full many a mile.

She, like the fragrant violet,
  Still flourish'd in her native mead:
He, like the stream, improving yet
  The further from his fountain-head.

The ſtream muſt now no further ſtray;
  A fountain fix'd by Venus' power
In his clear boſom, to diſplay
  The beauties of his bord'ring flower.

When gracious Anna did unite
  Two jarring nations into one,
She bade them mutually unite,
  And make each other's good their own.

Henceforth let each returning year
  The *roſe* and *thiſtle* bear one ſtem :
The *thiſtle* be the *roſe's* ſpear,
  The *roſe* the *thiſtle's* diadem.

The queen of Britain's high decree,
  The queen of love is bound to keep;
Anna, the ſovereign of the ſea,
  Venus, the daughter of the deep.   W. B.

ODE.
To Mrs. A. R.

Tune—*Love's goddeſs in a myrtle grove.*

NOW ſpring begins her ſmiling round,
  And laviſh paints th' enamell'd ground;
The birds now lift their chearful voice,
And gay on every bough rejoice :
The lovely *graces* hand in hand
Knit faſt in love's eternal band,
With early ſtep, at morning-dawn,
Tread lightly o'er the dewy lawn.

Where'er the youthful *ſiſters* move,
They fire the ſoul to genial love :
Now, by the river's painted ſide,
The ſwain delights his country-bride ;

While pleas'd, she hears his artless vows,
Each bird his feather'd confort wooes:
Soon will the ripen'd summer yield
Her various gifts to every field.

The fertile trees, a lovely show!
With ruby-tinctur'd birth shall glow;
Sweet smells, from beds of lilies born,
Perfume the breezes of the morn:
The smiling day and dewy night
To rural scenes my fair invite;
With summer sweets to feast her eye,
Yet soon, soon, will the summer fly.

Attend, my lovely maid, and know
To profit by th' instructive show.
Now young and blooming thou appears,
All in the flourish of thy years:
The lovely bud shall soon disclose
To every eye the blushing rose;
Now, now the tender stalk is seen
With beauty fresh, and ever green.

But when the sunny hours are past,
Think not the coz'ning scene will last;
Let not the flatt'rer hope persuade,
Ah! must I say, that it will fade?
For see the summer flies away,
Sad emblem of our own decay!
Now winter from the frozen north
Drives swift his iron chariot forth.

His grizly hands in icy chains
Fair 'Tweda's silver stream constrains.
Cast up thy eyes, how bleak and bare
He wanders on the tops of Yare;
Behold his footsteps dire are seen
Confess'd o'er ev'ry with'ring green;
Griev'd at the sight, when thou shalt see
A snowy wreath to clothe each tree.

Frequenting now the stream no more,
Thou flies, displeas'd, the frozen shore,
When thou shalt miss the flowers that grew
But late, to charm thy ravish'd view;
Then shall a sigh thy soul invade,
And o'er thy pleasures cast a shade:
Shall I, ah! horrid! wilt thou say,
Be like to this some other day?

Yet when in snow and dreary frost
The pleasure of the fields is lost,
To blazing hearths at home we run,
And fires supply the distant sun;
In gay delights our hours employ,
And do not lose, but change our joy.
Happy! abandon every care,
To lead the dance, to court the fair.

To turn the page of sacred bards,
To drain the bowl, and deal the cards.
In cities thus, with witty friends,
In smiles the hoary season ends.
But when the lovely white and red
From the pale ashy cheek is fled,
Then wrinkles dire, and age severe,
Make beauty fly, we know not where.

The fair, whom fates unkind disarm,
Ah! must they never cease to charm?
Or is there left some *pleasing art*
To keep secure a captive heart?
Unhappy love! may lovers say,
Beauty, thy food, does swift decay;
When once that short-liv'd flock is spent,
What is't thy famine can prevent?

Lay in good sense with timeous care,
That love may live on wisdom's fare:
Though *ecstasy* with *beauty* flies,
Esteem is born when beauty dies.

Happy the man whom fates decree
Their richeſt gift in giving thee;
Thy beauty ſhall his youth engage,
Thy wiſdom ſhall delight his age.

Horace, Book I. Ode II.
To W. D.

Tune—Willy was a wanton wag.

WILLY, ne'er enquire what end
    The gods for thee or me intend;
How vain the ſearch, that but beſtows
The knowledge of our future woes!
Happier the man that ne'er repines,
Whatever lot his fate aſſigns,
Than they that idly vex their lives
With wizards and inchanting wives.

Thy preſent years in mirth employ,
And conſecrate thy youth to joy;
Whether the fates to thy old ſcore
Shall bounteous add a winter more,
Or this ſhall lay thee cold in earth
That rages o'er the Pentland firth,
No more with Home the dance to lead:
Take my advice, ne'er vex thy head.

With blyth intent the goblet pour,
That's ſacred to the genial hour,
In flowing wine ſtill warm thy ſoul,
And have no thoughts beyond the bowl.
Behold, the flying hour is loſt,
For time rides ever on the poſt,
Even while we ſpeak, even while we think,
And waits not for the ſtanding drink.

Collect thy joys each present day,
And live in youth, while best you may;
Have all your pleasures at command,
Nor trust one day in fortune's hand.
Then, Willy, be a wanton wag,
If ye wad please the lasses braw,
At bridals then ye'll bear the brag,
And carry ay the gree awa'.

✤✤✤✤✤✤✤✤✤✤✤✤✤✤✤✤✤✤✤✤✤✤✤✤✤✤✤✤✤✤✤✤✤✤✤✤✤✤✤

The Widow.

THE widow can bake, and the widow can brew,
    The widow can shape, and the widow can few,
And mony braw things the widow can do;
    Then have at the widow, my laddie.
With courage attack her baith early and late,
To kifs her and clap her, you manna be blate,
Speak well, and do better, for that's the best gate
    To win a young widow, my laddie.

The widow she's youthfu', and never ae hair
The war of the wearing, and has a good skair
Of everything lovely; she's witty and fair,
    And has a rich jointure, my laddie.
What cou'd you wish better your pleasure to crown,
Than a widow, the bonniest toast in the town,
With naething, but draw in your stool and sit down,
    And sport with the widow, my laddie?

Then till'er, and kill'er with courtesy dead,
Tho' stark love and kindnefs be all ye can plead;
Be heartsome and airy, and hope to succeed
    With a bonny gay widow, my laddie.
Strike iron while it's het, if ye'd have it to wald,
For fortune ay favours the active and bauld,
But ruins the wooer that's thowlefs and cauld,
    Unfit for the widow, my laddie.

The Highland Lassie.

THE lawland maids gang trig and fine,
    But aft they'r four and unco faucy;
Sae proud, they never can be kind,
    Like my good-humour'd highland laffie.
O my bonny, bonny highland laffie,
My hearty fmiling highland laffie,
May never care make thee lefs fair,
But bloom of youth ftill blefs my laffie.

Than ony lafs in borrows town,
    Wha mak their cheeks with patches mottie,
I'd tak my Katy but a gown,
    Bare-footed in her little coatie.
O my bonny, &c.

Beneath the brier or brecken bufh,
    Whene'er I kifs and court my dautie,
Happy and blyth as ane wad wifh,
    My flightern heart gangs pittie-pattie.
O my bonnie, &c.

O'er higheft heathery hills I'll ftenn
    With cockit gun and ratches tenty,
To drive the deer out of their den,
    To feaft my lafs on difhes dainty.
O my bonny, &c.

There's nane fhall dare by deed or word
    'Gainft her to wag a tongue or finger,
While I can wield my trufty fword,
    Or frae my fide whifk out a whinger.
O my bonny, &c.

The mountains clad with purple bloom
    And berries ripe, invite my treafure
To range with me, let great folk gloom,
    While wealth and pride confound their pleafure.

O my bonny, bonny highland laſſie,
My lovely ſmiling highland laſſie,
May never care make thee leſs fair,
But bloom of youth ſtill bleſs my laſſie.

Jocky blyth and gay.

BLYTH Jocky young and gay,
   Is all my heart's delight;
He's all my talk by day,
   And all my dreams by night.
     If from the lad I be,
     'Tis winter then with me;
     But when he tarries here,
     'Tis ſummer all the year.

When I and Jocky met
   Firſt on the flow'ry dale,
Right ſweetly he me treat,
   And love was all his tale.
     You are the laſs, ſaid he,
     That ſtaw my heart frae me;
     O eaſe me of my pain,
     And never ſhaw diſdain.

Well can my Jocky kyth
   His love and courteſie,
He made my heart full blyth
   When he firſt ſpake to me.
     His ſuit I ill deny'd,
     He kiſs'd, and I comply'd:
     Sae Jocky promis'd me,
     That he wad faithful be.

I'm glad when Jocky comes,
   Sad when he gangs away;
'Tis night when Jocky glooms,
   But when he ſmiles 'tis day.

When our eyes meet, I pant,
I colour, figh, and faint;
What lafs that wad be kind,
Can better tell her mind?   Q.

Had away from me DONALD.

O COME away, come away,
   Come away wi' me, Jenny;
Sic frowns I canna bear frae ane
   Whafe fmiles anes ravifh'd me, Jenny;
If you'll be kind, you'll never find
   That ought fall alter me, Jenny;
For your the miftrefs of my mind,
   Whate'er you think of me, Jenny.

Firft when your fweets enflav'd my heart,
   You feem'd to favour me, Jenny;
But now, alas! you act a part
   That fpeaks unconftancy, Jenny;
Unconftancy is fic a vice,
   'Tis not befitting thee, Jenny;
It fuits not with your virtue nice
   To carry fae to me, Jenny.

Her ANSWER.

O HAD away, had away,
   Had away frae me, Donald;
Your heart is made o'er large for ane,
   It is not meet for me, Donald:
Some fickle miftrefs you may find
   Will jilt as faft as thee, Donald;
To ilka fwain fhe will prove kind,
   And nae lefs kind to thee, Donald.

But I've a heart that's naething fuch,
    'Tis fill'd with honefty, Donald,
I'll ne'er love money, I'll love much,
    I hate all levity, Donald.
Therefore nae mair, with art, pretend
    Your heart is chain'd to mine, Donald;
For words of falfhood ill defend
    A roving love like thine, Donald.

Firft when you courted, I muft own
    I frankly favour'd you, Donald;
Apparent worth and fair renown
    Made me believe you true, Donald.
Ilk virtue then feem'd to adorn
    The man efteem'd by me, Donald;
But now, the mafk fall'n aff, I fcorn
    To ware a thought on thee, Donald.

And now, for ever, had away,
    Had away from me, Donald;
Gae feek a heart that's like your ain,
    And come nae mair to me, Donald;
For I'll referve myfell for ane,
    For ane that's liker me, Donald;
If fic a ane I canna find,
    I'll ne'er loo man, nor thee, Donald.

DONALD.

Then I'm thy man, and falfe report
    Has only tald a lie, Jenny;
To try thy truth, and make us fport,
    The tale was rais'd by me, Jenny.

JENNY.

When this ye prove, and ftill can love,
    Then come away to me, Donald;
I'm well content, ne'er to repent
    That I have fmil'd on thee, Donald.

Todlen butt, and todlen ben.

WHEN I've a faxpence under my thumb,
  Then I'll get credit in ilka town:
But ay when I'm poor they bid me gang by;
O! poverty parts good company.
  Todlen hame, todlen hame,
  Cou'dna my loove come todlen hame?

Fair fa' the goodwife, and fend her good fale,
She gies us white bannocks to drink her ale,
Syne if that her tippony chance to be fma',
We'll tak a good fcour o't, and ca't awa'.
  Todlen hame, todlen hame,
  As round as a neep come todlen hame.

My kimmer and I lay down to fleep,
And twa pint-ftoups at our bed's feet;
And ay when we waken'd, we drank them dry:
What think ye of my wee kimmer and I?
  Todlen butt, and todlen ben,
  Sae round as my loove comes todlen hame.

Leez me on liquor, my todlen dow,
Ye're ay fae good-humour'd when weeting your mou;
When fober, fae four, ye'll fight with a flee,
That 'tis a blyth fight to the bairns and me,
  When todlen hame, todlen hame,
  When round as a neep you come todlen hame.   Z.

The auld Man's beft Argument.

Tune—*Widow, are ye wawkin?*

O WHA's that at my chamber door?
  "Fair widow, are ye wawkin?"
Auld carl, your fuit give o'er,
  Your love lies a' in tawking.

Gi'e me a lad that's young and tight,
    Sweet like an April meadow;
'Tis fic as he can blefs the fight
    And bofom of a widow.

"O widow, wilt thou let me in,
    I'm pawky, wife, and thrifty,
And come of a right gentle kin,
    I'm little mair than fifty."
Daft carl dit your mouth,
    What fignifies how pawky,
Or gentle born ye be,—bot youth?
    In love you're but a gawky.

"Then, widow, let thefe guineas fpeak,
    That powerfully plead clinkan,
And if they fail, my mouth I'll fleek,
    And nae mair love will think on."
Thefe court indeed, I maun confefs,
    I think they make you young, Sir,
And ten times better can exprefs
    Affection, than your tongue, Sir.

The peremptor Lover.

Tune—*John Anderfon, my jo.*

'TIS not your beauty, nor your wit,
    That can my heart obtain;
For they cou'd never conquer yet,
    Either my breaft or brain:
For if you'll not prove kind to me,
    And true as heretofore,
Henceforth I'll fcorn your flave to be,
    Or doat upon you more.

Think not my fancy to o'ercome,
    By proving thus unkind;
No smoothed sight, nor smiling frown,
    Can satisfy my mind.
Pray let Platonicks play such pranks,
    Such follies I deride;
For love, at least, I will have thanks,
    And something else beside.

Then open-hearted be with me,
    As I shall be with you,
And let our actions be as free
    As virtue will allow.
If you'll prove loving, I'll prove kind,
    If true, I'll constant be;
If fortune chance to change your mind,
    I'll turn as soon as you.

Since our affections well ye know,
    In equal terms do stand,
'Tis in your power to love or no,
    Mine's likewise in my hand.
Dispense with your austerity,
    Unconstancy abhor,
Or, by great Cupid's deity,
    I'll never love you more.   Q.

What's that to you?

Tune—*The glancing of her apron.*

MY Jeany and I have toil'd
    The live lang summer-day,
Till we almost were spoil'd
    At making of the hay:

Her kurchy was of holland clear,
    Ty'd on her bonny brow,
I whifper'd fomething in her ear;
    But what's that to you?

Her ftockings were of Kerfey green,
    As tight as ony filk:
O fic a leg was never feen,
    Her fkin was white as milk:
Her hair was black as ane could wifh,
    And fweet, fweet was her mou,
Oh! Jeany daintily can kifs;
    But what's that to you?

The rofe and lily baith combine
    To make my Jeany fair,
There is nae bennifon like mine,
    I have amaift nae care;
Only I fear my Jeany's face
    May caufe mae men to rue,
And that may gar me fay, alas!
    But what's that to you?

Conceal thy beauties if thou can,
    Hide that fweet face of thine,
That I may only be the man
    Enjoys thefe looks divine.
O do not proftitute, my dear,
    Wonders to common view,
And I with faithful heart fhall fwear,
    For ever to be true.

King Solomon had wives enow,
    And mony a concubine;
But I enjoy a blifs mair true,
    His joys were fhort of mine;
And Jeany's happier than they,
    She feldom wants her due;
All debts of love to her I pay,
    And what's that to you?

                                        Q.

SONG.

To the absent FLORINDA.

Tune—*Queen of Sheba's March.*

COME, Florinda, lovely charmer,
    Come and fix this wav'ring heart;
Let those eyes my soul rekindle,
    Ere I feel some foreign dart.

Come, and with thy smiles secure me,
    If this heart be worth thy care,
Favour'd by my dear Florinda,
    I'll be true, as she is fair.

Thousand beauties trip around me,
    And my yielding breast assail;
Come and take me to thy bosom,
    Ere my constant passion fail.

Come, and like the radiant morning,
    On my soul serenely shine,
Then those glimmering stars shall vanish,
    Lost in splendour more divine.

Long this heart has been thy victim,
    Long has felt the pleasing pain,
Come, and with an equal passion
    Make it ever thine remain.

Then, my charmer, I can promise,
    If our souls in love agree,
None in all the upper dwellings
    Shall be happier than we.

A Bacchanal Song.

Tune—*Auld Sir Symon the King.*

COME here's to the nymph that I love!
    Away, ye vain sorrows, away:
Far, far from me, sorrows, begone,
    All there shall be pleasant and gay.

Far hence be the sad and the pensive,
    Come fill up the glasses around,
We'll drink till our faces be ruddy,
    And all our vain sorrows are drown'd.

'Tis done, and my fancy's exulting,
    With every gay blooming desire,
My blood with brisk ardour is glowing,
    Soft pleasures my bosom inspire.

My soul now to love is dissolving,
    Oh fate! had I here my fair charmer,
I'd clasp her, I'd clasp her so eager,
    Of all her disdain I'd disarm her.

But hold, what has love to do here,
    With his troops of vain cares in array?
Avaunt, idle pensive intruder,—
    He triumphs, he will not away.

I'll drown him, come, give me a bumper;
    Young Cupid, here's to thy confusion.—
Now, now he's departing, he's vanquish'd,
    Adieu to his anxious delusion.

Come, jolly god Bacchus, here's to thee;
    Huzza boys, huzza boys, huzza;
Sing Io, sing Io to Bacchus—
    Hence all ye dull thinkers, withdraw.

Come, what should we do but be jovial?
    Come tune up your voices and sing;
What soul is so dull to be heavy,
    When wine sets our fancies on wing?

Come, Pegasus lies in this bottle,
    He'll mount us, he'll mount us on high,
Each of us a gallant young Perseus,
    Sublime we'll ascend to the sky.

Come mount, or adieu, I arise,
    In seas of wide æther I'm drown'd;
The clouds far beneath me are sailing,
    I see the spheres whirling around.

What darkness, what rattling is this?
    Thro' Chaos' dark regions I'm hurl'd,
And now,—oh my head it is knock'd
    Upon some confounded new world.

Now, now these dark shades are retiring,
    See yonder bright blazes a star;
Where am I!—behold the Empyreum,
    With flaming light streaming from far.   I. W. Q.

SONG.

To Mrs. A. C.

Tune—*All in the Downs.*

WHEN beauty blazes heavenly bright,
    The muse can no more cease to sing
Than can the lark, with rising light,
    Her notes neglect with drooping wing.
The morning shines, harmonious birds mount high:
The dawning beauty smiles, and poets fly.

Young Annie's budding graces claim
  Th' infpired thought, and fofteft lays;
And kindle in the breaft a flame,
  Which muft be vented in her praife.
Tell us, ye gentle fhepherds, have you feen
E'er one fo like an angel tread the green?

Ye youth, be watchful of your hearts;
  When fhe appears, take the alarm:
Love on her beauty points his darts,
  And wings an arrow from each charm.
Around her eyes and fmiles the graces fport,
And to her fnowy neck and breaft refort.

But vain muft every caution prove:
  When fuch inchanting fweetnefs fhines,
The wounded fwain muft yield to love,
  And wonder, tho' he hopelefs pines.
Such flames the foppifh butterfly fhou'd fhun;
The eagle's only fit to view the fun.

She's as the op'ning lily fair;
  Her lovely features are complete;
Whilft heaven indulgent makes her fhare
  With angels all that's wife and fweet.
Thefe virtues which divinely deck her mind,
Exalt each other of th' inferior kind.

Whether fhe love the rural fcenes,
  Or fparkle in the airy town,
O! happy he her favour gains,
  Unhappy! if fhe on him frown.
The mufe unwilling quits the lovely theme,
Adieu fhe fings, and thrice repeats her name.

A Paſtoral Song.

Tune—*My apron, deary.*

JAMIE.

WHILE our flocks are a-feeding,
    And we're void of care,
Come, Sandy, let's tune
    To praiſe of the fair:
For, inſpir'd by my Suſie,
    I'll ſing in ſuch lays,
That Pan, were he judge,
    Muſt allow me the bays.

SANDY.

While under this hawthorn
    We ly at our eaſe,
By a muſical ſtream,
    And refreſh'd by the breeze
Of a zephyr ſo gentle,
    Yes, Jamie, I'll try
For to match you and Suſie,
    Dear Katie and I.

JAMIE.

Oh! my Suſie ſo lovely,
    She's without compare,
She's ſo comely, ſo good,
    And ſo charmingly fair:
Sure, the gods were at pains
    To make ſo complete
A nymph, that for love
    There was ne'er one ſo meet.

SANDY.

Oh my Katie's ſo bright,
    She's ſo witty and gay;
Love, join'd with the graces,
    Around her looks play.

In her mien she's so graceful,
   In her humour so free:
Sure the gods never fram'd
   A maid fairer than she.

JAMIE.

Had my Susie been there,
   When the shepherd declared
For the lady of Lemnos,
   She had lost his regard:
And o'ercome by a presence
   More beauteously bright,
He had own'd her outdone,
   As the darkness by light.

SANDY.

Not fair Helen of Greece,
   Nor all the whole train,
Either of real beauties,
   Or those poets feign,
Cou'd be match'd with my Katie,
   Whose ev'ry sweet charm
May conquer best judges,
   And coldest hearts warm.

JAMIE.

Neither riches nor honour,
   Or any thing great,
Do I ask of the gods,
   But that this be my fate,
That my Susie to all
   My kind wishes comply:
For with her wou'd I live,
   And with her I wou'd die.

SANDY.

If the fates give me Katie,
   And her I enjoy,

I have all my defires;
    Nought can me annoy:
For my charmer has ev'ry
    Delight in fuch ftore,
She'll make me more happy
    Than fwain e'er before.

Love will find out the way.

OVER the mountains,
    And over the waves,
Over the fountains,
    And under the graves:
Over the floods that are deepeft,
    Which do Neptune obey;
Over rocks that are fteepeft,
    Love will find out the way.

Where there is no place
    For the glow-worm to ly;
Where there is no fpace
    For the receipt of a fly;
Where the midge dare not venture,
    Left herfelf faft fhe lay:
But if love come, he will enter,
    And foon find out his way.

You may efteem him
    A child in his force;
Or you may deem him
    A coward, which is worfe:
But if fhe, whom love doth honour,
    Be conceal'd from the day,
Set a thoufand guards upon her,
    Love will find out the way.

Some think to lose him,
    Which is too unkind;
And some do suppose him,
    Poor thing, to be blind;
But if ne'er so close ye wall him,
    Do the best that ye may,
Blind love, if so ye call him,
    He will find out the way.

You may train the eagle
    To stoop to your fist;
Or you may inveigle
    The Phœnix of the east;
The lioness, ye may move her
    To give o'er her prey:
But you'll never stop a lover,
    He will find out his way.

SONG.

Tune—*Throw the wood, laddie.*

AS early I walk'd, on the first of sweet May,
    Beneath a steep mountain,
    Beside a clear fountain,
I heard a grave lute soft melody play,
Whilst the echo resounded the dolorous lay.

I listen'd, and look'd, and spy'd a young swain,
    With aspect distressed,
    And spirits oppressed,
Seem'd clearing afresh, like the sky after rain,
And thus he discover'd how he strave with his pain.

Tho' Elisa be coy, why shou'd I repine,
    That a maid much above me,
    Vouchsafes not to love me?
In her high sphere of worth I never could shine;
Then why should I seek to debase her to mine?

No: henceforth esteem shall govern my desire,
      And, in due subjection,
        Retain warm affection;
To shew that self-love inflames not my fire,
And that no other swain can more humbly admire.

When passion shall cease to rage in my breast,
      Then quiet returning,
        Shall hush my sad mourning;
And, lord of myself, in absolute rest,
I'll hug the condition which heav'n shall think best.

Thus friendship unmix'd, and wholly refin'd,
      May still be respected,
        Tho' love is rejected:
Elisa shall own, tho' to love not inclin'd,
That she ne'er had a friend like her lover resign'd.

May the fortunate youth who hereafter shall woo
      With prosp'rous endeavour,
        And gain her dear favour,
Know, as well as I, what t' Elisa is due,
Be much more deserving, but never less true.

Whilst I, disengag'd from all amorous cares,
      Sweet liberty tasting,
        On calmest peace feasting,
Employing my reason to dry up my tears,
In hopes of heav'n's blisses I'll spend my few years.

Ye pow'rs, that preside o'er virtuous love,
      Come aid me with patience,
        To bear my vexations;
With equal desires my flutt'ring heart move,
With sentiments purest my notions improve.

If love in his fetters e'er catch me again,
      May courage protect me,
        And prudence direct me;
Prepar'd for all fates, rememb'ring the swain,
Who grew happily wife, after loving in vain.

Rob's Jock. A very auld Ballat.

Rob's Jock came to woo our Jenny,
    On ae feaſt-day when we were fou;
She brankit faſt and made her bonny,
    And ſaid, Jock, come ye here to woo?
    She burniſt her baith breaſt and brou,
And made her clear as ony cloak:
    Then ſpake her dame, and ſaid, I trou
Ye come to woo our Jenny, Jock.

Jock ſaid, Forſuith, I yern fu' fain
    To luk my head, and ſit down by you:
Then ſpak her minny, and ſaid again,
    My bairn has tocher enough to gi'e you.
Tehie! quo' Jenny, kick, kick, I ſee you:
Minny, yon man makes but a mock.
    Deil hae the liers—fu lies me o' you,
I come to woo your Jenny, quo' Jock.—

My bairn has tocher of her awin:
    A guſe, a gryce, a cock and hen,
A ſtirk, a ſtaig, an acre ſawin,
    A bakbread and a bannock-ſtane;
    A pig, a pot, and a kirn there-ben,
A kame but a kaming-ſtock;
    With coags and luggies nine or ten:
Come ye to woo our Jenny, Jock?

A wecht, a peat-creel, and a cradle,
    A pair of clips, a graip, a flail,
An ark, an ambray, and a ladle,
    A milſie, and a ſowen-pail,
    A rouſty whittle to ſhear the kail,
And a timber mell the bear to knock,
    Twa ſhelfs made of an auld fir dale:
Come ye to woo our Jenny, Jock?

A furm, a furlet, and a peck,
    A rock, a reel, and a wheel-band,
A tub, a barrow, and a feck,
    A fpurtil-braid, and an elwand.
    Then Jock took Jenny be the hand,
And cry'd a feaft! and flew a cock,
    And made a bridle upo' land,
Now I have got your Jenny, quo' Jock.

Now dame I have your daughter marri'd,
    And tho' ye mak it ne'er fae tough,
I let you wit fhe's nae mifcarried,
    It's we'll kend I have gear enough:
    Ane auld gaw'd gloyd fell o'er a heugh,
A fpade, a fpit, a fpur, a fock;
    Withouten owfen I have a plough:
May that no fer your Jenny? quo' Jock.

A treen truncher, a ram-horn fpoon,
    Twa buits of barkit, blafint leather,
A graith that ganes to coble fhoon,
    And a thrawcruik to twyne a teather,
    Twa crocks that moup amang the heather,
A pair of branks, and a fetter lock,
    A teugh purfe made of a fwine's blather,
To had your tocher, Jenny, quo' Jock.

Good elding for our winter-fire,
    A cod of caff wad fill a cradle,
A rake of iron to clat the bire,
    A deuk about the dubs to paddle,
    The pannel of an auld led-faddle,
And Rob my eem heckt me a flock,
    Twa lufty lips to lick a laddle.
May thir no gain your Jenny? quo' Jock.

A pair of hames and brechom fine,
    And without bitts a bridle-renzie,
A fark made of the linkome twine,
    A gay green cloak that will not ftenzie;

  Mair yet in ftore, I needna fenzie,
  Five hundred flaes, a fendy flock;
   And are not thae a wakrife menzie,
  To gae to bed with Jenny and Jock?

 Tak thir for my part of the feaft,
  It is well knawin I am well bodin:
 Ye need not fay my part is leaft,
  Wer they as meikle as they'r lodin.
  The wife fpeer'd gin the kail were fodin,
 When we have done, tak hame the brock;
  The roft was teugh as raploch hodin,
 With which they feafted Jenny and Jock. Z.

SONG.

Tune—A rock and a wee pickle tow.

I HAVE a green purfe, and a wee pickle gowd,
 A bonny piece land and planting on't,
It fattens my flocks, and my bairns it has flow'd;
 But the beft thing of a's yet wanting on't.
   To grace it, and trace it,
   And gie me delight;
   To blefs me, and kifs me,
   And comfort my fight,
With beauty by day, and kindnefs by night,
 And nae mair my lane gang fauntring on't.

My Chrifty fhe's charming and good as fhe's fair;
 Her een and her mouth are inchanting fweet,
She fmiles me on fire, her frowns gie defpair:
 I love while my heart gaes panting wi't.
   Thou faireft, and deareft,
   Delight of my mind,
   Whofe gracious embraces
   By heaven were defigned
For happieft tranfports, and bleffes refin'd,
 Nae langer delay thy granting fweet.

For thee, bonny Chrifty, my fhepherds and hinds
  Shall carefully make the year's dainties thine :
Thus freed frae laigh care, while love fills our minds,
  Our days fhall with pleafure and plenty fhine.
      Then hear me, and chear me
        With fmiling confent,
      Believe me, and give me
        No caufe to lament,
Since I ne'er can be happy, till thou fay, *Content,*
  I'm pleas'd with my Jamie, *and he fhall be mine.*

SONG.

To its ain tune.

ALTHO' I be but a country-lafs,
  Yet a lofty mind I bear—O,
And think myfell as good as thofe
  That rich apparel wear—O.
Altho' my gown be hame-fpun grey,
  My fkin it is as faft—O.
As them that fattin weeds do wear,
  And carry their heads aloft—O.

What tho' I keep my father's fheep,
  The thing that muft be done—O,
With garlands of the fineft flowers,
  To fhade me frae the fun—O.
When they are feeding pleafantly,
  Where grafs and flowers do fpring—O,
Then on a flowery bank at noon,
  I fet me down and fing—O.

My Paifly piggy, cork'd with fage,
  Contains my drink but thin—O ;
No wines do e'er my brains enrage,
  Or tempt my mind to fin—O.

My country-curds, and wooden fpoon,
  I think them unco fine—O,
And on a flowery bank at noon,
  I fet me down and dine—O.

Altho' my parents cannot raife
  Great bags of fhining gold—O,
Like them whafe daughters, now a-days,
  Like fwine are bought and fold—O;
Yet my fair body it fhall keep
  An honeft heart within—O;
And for twice fifty thoufand crowns,
  I value not a prin—O.

I ufe nae gums upon my hair,
  Nor chains about my neck—O,
Nor fhining rings upon my hands,
  My fingers ftreight to deck—O;
But for that lad to me fhall fa',
  And I have grace to wed—O,
I'll keep a Jewel worth them a',
  I mean my maidenhead—O.

If canny fortune give to me
  The man I dearly love—O,
Tho' we want gear, I dinna care,
  My hands I can improve—O,
Expecting for a bleffing ftill
  Defcending from above—O,
Then we'll embrace, and fweetly kifs,
  Repeating tales of love—O.

Waly, waly, gin love be bonny.

O WALY, waly up the bank,
    And waly, waly down the brae,
And waly, waly yon burn-fide,
    Where I and my love wont to gae.
I lean'd my back unto an aik,
    I thought it was a trufty tree,
But firft it bow'd, and fyne it brak,
    Sae my true love did lightly me.

O waly, waly, but love be bonny,
    A little time while it is new,
But when 'tis auld, it waxeth cauld,
    And fades away like the morning-dew.
O wherefore fhould I bufk my head?
    Or wherefore fhou'd I kame my hair?
For my true love has me forfook,
    And fays he'll never love me mair.

Now Arthur-Seat fhall be my bed,
    The fheets fhall ne'er be fyl'd by me,
Saint Anton's well fhall be my drink,
    Since my true love has forfaken me.
Martinmas wind when wilt thou blaw,
    And fhake the green leaves off the tree?
O gentle death, when wilt thou come?
    For of my life I am weary.

'Tis not the froft that freezes fell,
    Nor blawing fnaw's inclemency:
'Tis not fic cauld that makes me cry,
    But my love's heart grown cauld to me.
When we came in by Glafgow town,
    We were a comely fight to fee;
My love was clad in the black velvet,
    And I myfell in cramafie.

But had I wift before I kifs'd,
    That love had been fae ill to win,
I'd lock'd my heart in a cafe of gold,
    And pinn'd it with a filver pin.
Oh, oh! if my young babe were born,
    And fet upon the nurfe's knee,
And I myfell were dead and gane,
    For a maid again I'll never be.   Z.

The loving Lafs and Spinning-Wheel.

AS I fat at my fpinning-wheel,
    A bonny lad was paffing by:
I view'd him round, and lik'd him weel,
For trouth he had a glancing eye.
    My heart new panting 'gan to feel,
    But ftill I turn'd my fpinning-wheel.

With looks all kindnefs he drew near,
And ftill mair lovely did appear;
And round about my flender wafte
He clafp'd his arms, and me embrac'd:
    To kifs my hand, fyne down did kneel,
    As I fat at my fpinning-wheel.

My milk-white hands he did extol,
And prais'd my fingers lang and fmall,
And faid there was nae lady fair
That ever cou'd with me compare.
    Thefe words into my heart did fteal,
    But ftill I turn'd my fpinning-wheel.

Altho' I feemingly did chide,
Yet he wad never be deny'd,
But ftill declar'd his love the mair,
Until my heart was wounded fair:
    That I my love cou'd fcarce conceal,
    Yet ftill I turn'd my fpinning-wheel.

My hanks of yarn, my rock and reel,
My winnels and my ſpinning-wheel;
He bid me leave them all with ſpeed,
And gang with him to yonder mead.
 My yielding heart ſtrange flames did feel,
 Yet ſtill I turn'd my ſpinning-wheel.

About my neck his arm he laid,
And whiſper'd, Riſe, my bonny maid,
And with me to yon hay-cock go,
I'll teach thee better wark to do.
 In troth I loo'd the motion weel,
 And loot alane my ſpinning-wheel.

Amang the pleaſing cocks of hay,
Then with my bonny lad I lay;
What laſſie, young and faſt as I,
Cou'd ſie a handſome lad deny?
 Theſe pleaſures I cannot reveal,
 That far ſurpaſt the ſpinning-wheel.

On the Marriage of the R. H. Lord G—— and Lady K—— C——.

SONG.

Tune—*The highland laddie.*

BRIGANTIUS.

NOW all thy virgin-ſweets are mine,
 And all the ſhining charms that grace thee:
My fair Melinda, come, recline
 Upon my breaſt, while I embrace thee,
And tell without diſſembling art,
 My happy raptures in thy boſom:
Thus will I plant within thy heart,
 A love that ſhall for ever bloſſom.

Chorus.

O the happy, happy, brave and bonny,
Sure the gods well pleas'd behold ye;
Their work admire, so great, so fair,
And well in all your joys uphold ye.

Melinda.

No more I blush, now that I'm thine,
    To own my love in transport tender,
Since that so brave a man is mine,
    To my Brigantius I surrender.
By sacred ties I'm now to move
    As thy exalted thoughts direct me;
And while my smiles engage thy love,
    Thy manly greatness shall protect me.

Chorus.

O the happy, &c.

Brigantius.

Soft fall thy words, like morning dew,
    New life on blowing flowers bestowing;
Thus kindly yielding makes me bow
    To heaven, with grateful spirit glowing.
My honour, courage, wealth, and wit,
    Thou dear delight, my chiefest treasure,
Shall be employ'd as thou thinks fit,
    As agents for our love and pleasure.

Chorus.

O the happy, &c.

Melinda.

With my Brigantius I could live
    In lonely cotts, beside a mountain,
And nature's easy wants relieve
    With shepherd's fare, and quaff the fountain.

What pleafes thee, the rural grove,
   Or congrefs of the fair and witty,
Shall give me pleafure with thy love,
   In plains retir'd, or focial city.

Chorus.

O the happy, &c.

Brigantius.

How fweetly canft thou charm my foul,
   O lovely fum of my defires!
Thy beauties all my cares controul,
   Thy virtue all that's good infpires.
Tune every inftrument of found,
   Which all thy mind divinely raifes,
Till every height and dale rebounds,
   Both loud and fweet, my darling's praifes.

Chorus.

O the happy, &c.

Melinda.

Thy love gives me the brighteft fhine,
   My happinefs is now completed,
Since all that's generous, great, and fine,
   In my Brigantius is united;
For which I'll ftudy thy delight,
   With kindly tale the time beguiling,
And round the change of day and night,
   Fix throughout life a conftant fmiling.

Chorus.

O the happy, &c.

SONG.

Tune— Wo's my heart that we should funder.

ADIEU, ye pleasant sports and plays,
    Farewell each song that was diverting;
Love tunes my pipe to mournful lays,
    I sing of Delia and Damon's parting.

Long had he lov'd, and long conceal'd
    The dear, tormenting, pleasant passion,
Till Delia's mildness had prevail'd
    On him to shew his inclination.

Just as the fair one seem'd to give
    A patient ear to his love story,
Damon must his Delia leave,
    To go in quest of toilsome glory.

Half-spoken words hung on his tongue,
    Their eyes refus'd the usual meeting;
And sighs supply'd their wonted song,
    These charming souls were chang'd to weeping.

Dear idol of my soul, adieu:
    Cease to lament, but ne'er to love me;
While Damon lives, he lives for you,
    No other charms shall ever move me.

Alas! who knows, when parted far
    From Delia, but you may deceive her?
The thought destroys my heart with care,
    Adieu, my dear, I fear, for ever.

If ever I forget my vows,
    May then my guardian angel leave me:
And more to aggravate my woes,
    Be you so good as to forgive me.   H.

O'er the hills and far away.

JOCKY met with Jenny fair,
    Aft be the dawning of the day;
But Jocky now is fu' of care,
Since Jenny ſtaw his heart away:
Altho' ſhe promis'd to be true,
She proven has, alake! unkind;
Which gars poor Jocky often rue,
That he e'er loo'd a fickle mind.
    And *it's o'er the hills and far away,*
        It's o'er the hills and far away,
        It's o'er the hills and far away,
    The wind has blawn my plaid away.

Now Jocky was a bonny lad,
As e'er was born in Scotland fair;
But now, poor man, he's e'en gane wood,
Since Jenny has gart him deſpair.
Young Jocky was a piper's ſon,
And fell in love when he was young;
But a' the ſprings that he cou'd play,
Was *o'er the hills and far away.*
    And *it's o'er the hills,* &c.

He ſung—when firſt my Jenny's face
I ſaw, ſhe ſeem'd fae fu' of grace,
With meikle joy my heart was fill'd,
That's now, alas! with ſorrow kill'd.
Oh! was ſhe but as true as fair,
'Twad put an end to my deſpair,
Inſtead of that ſhe is unkind,
And wavers like the winter wind.
    And *it's o'er the hills,* &c.

Ah! cou'd ſhe find the diſmal wae,
That for her ſake I undergae,
She cou'd nae chuſe but grant relief,
And put an end to a' my grief:

But oh! she is as fause as fair,
Which causes a' my sighs and care;
But she triumphs in proud disdain,
And takes a pleasure in my pain.
    And *it's o'er the hills*, &c.

Hard was my hap, to fa' in love
With ane that does sae faithless prove.
Hard was my fate to court a maid,
That has my constant heart betray'd.
A thousand times to me she sware,
She wad be true for evermair;
But, to my grief, alake, I say,
She staw my heart and ran away.
    And *it's o'er the hills*, &c.

Since that she will nae pity take,
I maun gae wander for her sake,
And, in ilk wood and gloomy grove,
I'll sighing sing, Adieu to love;
Since she is fause whom I adore,
I'll never trust a woman more;
Frae a' their charms I'll flee away,
And on my pipe I'll sweetly play,
   O'er hills and dales and far away,
   Out o'er the hills and far away,
   Out o'er the hills and far away,
   The wind has blawn my plaid away.   Z.

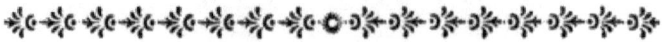

JENNY NETTLES.

SAW ye Jenny Nettles,
   Jenny Nettles, Jenny Nettles,
Saw ye Jenny Nettles
   Coming frae the market?

Bag and baggage on her back,
    Her fee and bountith in her lap;
Bag and baggage on her back,
    And a babie in her oxter?

I met ayont the kairny,
    Jenny Nettles, Jenny Nettles,
Singing till her bairny,
    Robin Rattle's baſtard;
To flee the dool upo' the ſtool,
    And ilka ane that mocks her,
She round about ſeeks Robin out,
    To ſtap it in his oxter.

Fy, fy! Robin Rattle,
    Robin Rattle, Robin Rattle;
Fy, fy! Robin Rattle,
    Uſe Jenny Nettles kindly:
Score out the blame, and ſhun the ſhame,
    And without mair debate o't,
Tak hame your wean, make Jenny fain
    The leel and leeſome gate o't.

Jocky's fou, and Jenny's fain.

JOCKY fou, Jenny fain,
    Jenny was nae ill to gain,
She was couthy, he was kind,
And thus the wooer tell'd his mind.

    Jenny, I'll nae mair be nice,
Gi'e me love at ony price;
I winna prig for red or whyt,
Love alane can gi'e delyt.

    Others ſeek they kenna what,
In looks, in carriage, and a' that;

Give me love, for her I court:
Love in love makes a' the sport.

Colours mingl'd unco fine,
Common motives lang sinsyne,
Never can engage my love,
Until my fancy first approve.

It is na meat, but appetite
That makes our eating a delyt;
Beauty is at best deceit;
Fancy only kens nae cheat. Q.

LEADER-HAUGHS and YARROW.

WHEN Phœbus bright the azure skies
　　With golden rays enlight'neth,
He makes all nature's beauties rise,
　　Herbs, trees, and flow'rs he quick'neth:
Amongst all those he makes his choice,
　　And with delight goes thorow,
With radiant beams and silver streams,
　　Are Leader-haughs and Yarrow.

When Aries the day and night
　　In equal length divideth,
Auld frosty Saturn takes his flight,
　　Nae langer he abideth:
Then Flora queen, with mantle green,
　　Casts aff her former sorrow,
And vows to dwell with Ceres sell
　　In Leader-haughs and Yarrow.

Pan playing on his aiten reed,
　　And shepherds him attending,
Do here resort their flocks to feed,
　　The hills and haughs commending;

With cur and kent upon the bent,
  Sing to the fun, Good-morrow,
And fwear nae fields mair pleafures yield
  Than Leader-haughs and Yarrow.

An houfe there ftands on Leader fide,
  Surmounting my defcriving,
With rooms fae rare, and windows fair,
  Like Dedalus' contriving :
Men paffing by, do aften cry,
  In footh it hath nae marrow;
It ftands as fweet on Leader fide,
  As Newark does on Yarrow.

A mile below, wha lifts to ride,
  They'll hear the mavis finging;
Into St. Leonard's banks fhe'll bide,
  Sweet birks her head o'er-hinging :
The lintwhite loud, and progne proud,
  With tuneful throats and narrow,
Into St. Leonard's banks they fing,
  As fweetly as in Yarrow.

The lapwing lilteth o'er the lee,
  With nimble wing fhe fporteth.
By vows fhe'll flee far frae the tree
  Where Philomel reforteth :
By break of day, the lark can fay,
  I'll bid you a good-morrow,
I'll ftreek my wing, and mounting fing,
  O'er Leader-haughs and Yarrow.

Park, Wanton-waws, and Wooden-cleugh,
  The eaft and weftern Mainfes,
The wood of Lauder's fair enough,
  The corns are good in Blainfhes,
Where aits are fine, and fald be kind,
  That if ye fearch all thorow
Mearns, Buchan, Mar, nane better are
  Than Leader-haughs and Yarrow.

In Burn Mill-bog and Whitflade fhaws,
    The fearful hare fhe haunteth,
Brig-haugh and Braidwoodfheil fhe knaws,
    And Chapel-wood frequenteth.
Yet when fhe irks, to Kaidfly birks
    She rins, and fighs for forrow,
That fhe fhould leave fweet Leader-haughs,
    And cannot win to Yarrow.

What fweeter mufic wad ye hear,
    Than hounds and beigles crying?
The ftarted hare rins hard with fear,
    Upon her fpeed relying.
But yet her ftrength it fails at length,
    Nae beilding can fhe borrow
In Sorrel's field, Cleckman or Hag's,
    And fighs to be in Yarrow.

For Rockwood, Ringwood, Spoty, Shag,
    With fight and fcent purfue her,
Till ah! her pith begins to flag,
    Nae cunning can refcue her.
O'er dub and dyke, o'er feugh and fyke,
    She'll run the fields all thorow,
Till fail'd fhe fa's in Leader-haughs,
    And bids farewell to Yarrow.

Sing Erflington and Cowden-knows,
    Where Homes had anes commanding:
And Drygrange with thy milk-white ewes,
    'Twixt Tweed and Leader ftanding:
The bird that flies through Reedpath trees,
    And Gledfwood banks ilk morrow,
May chant and fing, Sweet Leader-haughs,
    And bonny howms of Yarrow.

But minftrel Burn cannot affwage
    His grief, while life endureth,
To fee the changes of this age,
    That fleeting time procureth;

For mony a place ftands in hard cafe,
  Where blyth fowk kend nae forrow,
With Homes that dwelt on Leader fide,
  And Scots that dwelt on Yarrow.

For the fake of Somebody.

FOR the fake of fomebody,
  For the fake of fomebody,
I cou'd wake a winter-night,
  For the fake of fomebody:
I am gawn to feek a wife,
  I am gawn to buy a plaidy;
I have three flane of woo,
  Carling, is thy daughter ready?
For the fake of fomebody, &c.

Betty, laffie, fay't thy fell,
  Tho' thy dame be ill to fhoo,
Firft we'll buckle, then we'll tell,
  Let her flyte and fyne come too:
What fignifies a mither's gloom,
  When love in kiffes come in play?
Shou'd we wither in our bloom,
  And in fimmer mak nae hay?
For the fake, &c.

SHE.

Bonny lad, I care na by,
  Tho' I try my luck with thee,
Since ye are content to tye
  The ha'f-mark bridal band wi' me;
I'll flip hame, and wafh my feet,
  And fteal on linens fair and clean,
Syne at the tryfting-place we'll meet,
  To do but what my dame has done.
For the fake, &c.

HE.

Now my lovely Betty gives
　　Confent in fic a heartfome gate,
It me frae a' my care relieves,
　　And doubts that gart me aft look blate;
Then let us gang and get the grace,
　　For they that have an appetite
Shou'd eat;—and lovers fhou'd embrace;
　　If thefe be faults, 'tis nature's wyte.
For the fake, &c.

Norland Jocky and Southland Jenny.

A SOUTHLAND Jenny that was right bonny,
　　Had for a fuitor a norland Jonny;
But he was fican a bafhfu' wooer,
That he cou'd fcarcely fpeak unto her,
Till blinks of her beauty, and hopes o' her filler,
Forc'd him at laft to tell his mind till her.
My dear, quoth he, we'll nae langer tarry,
Gin ye can loo me, let's o'er the moor and marry.

SHE.

Come, come away then, my norland laddie,
Tho' we gang neatly, fome are mair gaudy;
And albeit I have neither gowd nor money,
Come and I'll ware my beauty on thee.

HE.

Ye laffes of the fouth, ye're a' for dreffing;
Laffes of the north mind milking and threfhing:
My minny wad be angry, and fae wad my daddy,
Shou'd I marry ane as dink as a lady.
For I maun hae a wife that will rife in the morning,
Crudle a' the milk, and keep the houfe a-fcaulding,
Toolie with her nibours, and learn at my minny,
A norland Jocky maun hae a norland Jenny.

SHE.

My father's only daughter and twenty thoufand pound,
Shall never be beftow'd on fic a filly clown;
For a' that I faid was to try what was in ye,
Gae hame, ye norland Jock, and court your norland
    Jenny.   Z.

The auld yellow-hair'd Laddie.

THE yellow-hair'd laddie fat down on yon brae,
    Cries, Milk the ews, laffie, let nane of them gae;
And ay fhe milked, and ay fhe fang,
The yellow-hair'd laddie fhall be my goodman.
And ay fhe milked, &c.

The weather is cauld, and my claithing is thin;
The ews are new clipped, they winna bught in:
They winna bught in tho' I fhould die,
O yellow-hair'd laddie, be kind to me:
They winna bught in, &c.

The goodwife cries butt the houfe, Jenny, come ben,
The cheefe is to mak, and the butter's to kirn.
Tho' butter, and cheefe, and a' fhou'd four,
I'll crack and kifs wi' my love ae ha'f-hour;
It's ae ha'f-hour, and we's e'en make it three,
For the yellow-hair'd laddie my hufband fhall be.

SONG.

Tune—BOOTH's *Minuet.*

FAIR, fweet, and young, receive a prize,
    Referv'd for your victorious eyes:
From crouds whom at your feet you fee,
Oh! pity, and diftinguifh me.

No graces can your form improve;
But all are loſt unleſs you love:
If that dear paſſion you diſdain,
Your charms and beauty are in vain.   X.

Part of an Epilogue, *ſung after the acting of the* Orphan *and* Gentle Shepherd *in* Taylors-hall, *by a ſet of young gentlemen,* Jan. 22, 1729.

Tune—*Beſſy Bell.*

THUS let's ſtudy night and day,
   To fit us for our ſtation,
That when we're men, we parts may play
   Are uſeful to our nation.
For now's the time, when we are young,
   To fix our views on merit,
Water its buds, and make the tongue
   And actions ſuit the ſpirit.

This all the fair and wiſe approve,
   We know it by your ſmiling,
And while we gain reſpect and love,
   Our ſtudies are not toiling.
Such application gives delight,
   And in the end proves gainful,
Tho' many a dark and lifeleſs wight
   May think it hard and painful.

Then never let us think our time
   And care, when thus employ'd,
Are thrown away, but deem't a crime,
   When youth's by ſloth deſtroy'd;
'Tis only active fouls can riſe
   To fame, and all that's ſplendid,
And favour in theſe conquering eyes,
   'Gainſt whom no heart's defended.

The generous Gentleman. A Sang.

Tune—*The bonny lafs of Brankfome.*

As I came in by Teviot-fide,
    And by the braes of Brankfome,
There firft I faw my bonnie bride,
    Young, fmiling, fweet, and handfome;
Her fkin was fafter than the down,
    And white as alabafter;
Her hair a fhining wavy brown,
    In ftraightnefs nane furpafs'd her:

Life glow'd upon her lip and cheek,
    Her clear een were furprifing,
And beautifully turn'd her neck,
    Her little breafts juft rifing:
Nae filken hofe, with goofhets fine,
    Or fhoon with glancing laces,
On her fair leg, forbade to fhine,
    Well fhapen native graces.

Ae little coat, and bodice white,
    Was fum of a' her claithing;
Even thae's o'er meikle; mair delyte
    She'd given cled with naething:
She lean'd upon a flow'ry brae,
    By which a burnie trotted;
On her I glower'd my faul away,
    While on her fweets I doted.

A thoufand beauties of defert
    Before had fcarce alarm'd me,
Till this dear artlefs ftruck my heart,
    And, bot defigning, charm'd me.
Hurry'd by love, clofe to my breaft
    I grafp'd this fund of bliffes;
Wha fmil'd, and faid, Without a prieft,
    Sir, hope for nought but kiffes.

I had nae heart to do her harm,
    And yet I cou'dna want her;
What she demanded, ilka charm
    Of her's pled, I shou'd grant her.
Since heaven had dealt to me a rowth,
    Straight to the kirk I led her,
There plighting her my faith and trowth,
    And a young lady made her.

The happy Clown.

HOW happy is the rural clown,
    Who, far remov'd from noise of town,
Contemns the glory of a crown,
    And in his safe retreat
Is pleased with his low degree,
Is rich in decent poverty,
From strife, from care and bus'ness free,
    At once baith good and great!

No drums disturb his morning sleep,
He fears no danger of the deep,
Nor noisy law, nor courts ne'er heap
    Vexation on his mind:
No trumpets rouse him to the war,
No hopes can bribe, no threats can dare;
From state intrigues he holds afar,
    And liveth unconfin'd.

Like those in golden ages born,
He labours gently to adorn
His small paternal fields of corn,
    And on their product feeds:
Each season of the wheeling year,
Industrious he improves with care;
And still some ripen'd fruits appear,
    So well his toil succeeds.

Now by a silver stream he lies,
And angles with his baits and flies,
And next the sylvan scene he tries,
   His spirit to regale :
Now from the rock or height he views
His fleecy flock, or teeming cows,
Then tunes his reed, or tries his muse,
   That waits his honest call.

Amidst his harmless easy joys,
No care his peace of mind destroys,
Nor does he pass his time in toys
   Beneath his just regard :
He's fond to feel the zephyr's breeze,
To plant and fned his tender trees :
And for attending well his bees,
   Enjoys the sweet reward.

The flow'ry meads, and silent coves,
The scenes of faithful rural loves,
And warbling birds on blooming groves,
   Afford a wish'd delight :
But O ! how pleasant is this life,
Bless'd with a chaste and virtuous wife,
And children prattling, void of strife,
   Around his fire at night.

Willy was a wanton Wag.

WILLY was a wanton wag,
   The blythest lad that e'er I saw,
At bridals still he bore the brag,
   And carried ay the gree awa :
His doublet was of Zetland shag,
   And wow ! but Willy he was braw,
And at his shouder hang a tag,
   That pleas'd the lasses best of a'.

He was a man without a clag,
    His heart was frank without a flaw;
And ay whatever Willy faid,
    It was ftill hadden as a law.
His boots they were made of the jag,
    When he went to the weapon-fhaw,
Upon the green nane durft him brag,
    The fiend a ane amang them a'.

And was not Willy well worth gowd?
    He wan the love of great and fma';
For after he the bride had kifs'd,
    He kifs'd the laffes hale-fale a'.
Sae merrily round the ring they row'd,
    When be the hand he led them a',
And fmack on fmack on them beftow'd,
    By virtue of a ftanding law.

And was na Willy a great lown,
    As fhyre a lick as e'er was feen?
When he danc'd with the laffes round,
    The bridegroom fpeer'd where he had been.
Quoth Willy, I've been at the ring,
    With bobbing, faith, my fhanks are fair;
Gae ca' your bride and maidens in,
    For Willy he dow do nae mair.

Then reft ye, Willy, I'll gae out,
    And for a wee fill up the ring.
But, fhame light on his fouple fnout,
    He wanted Willy's wanton fling.
Then ftraight he to the bride did fare,
    Says, Well's me on your bonny face,
With bobbing Willy's fhanks are fair,
    And I am come out to fill his place.

Bridegroom, fhe fays, you'll fpoil the dance,
    And at the ring you'll ay be lag,
Unlefs, like Willy, ye advance;
    (O! Willy has a wanton leg;)

For wi't he learns us a' to fteer,
  And foremoft ay bears up the ring;
We will find nae fic dancing here,
  If we want Willy's wanton fling.   W. W.

Celia's Reflections on herfelf for flighting Philander's Love.

Tune—The gallant fhoemaker.

YOUNG Philander woo'd me lang,
  But I was peevifh and forbad him,
I wadna' tent his loving fang;
  But now I wifh, I wifh I had him:
Ilk morning when I view my glafs,
  Then I perceive my beauty going;
And when the wrinkles feize the face,
  Then we may bid adieu to wooing.

My beauty, anes fo much admir'd,
  I find it fading faft, and flying,
My cheeks, which coral-like appear'd,
  Grow pale, the broken blood decaying.
Ah! we may fee ourfelves to be,
  Like fummer-fruit that is unfhaken;
When ripe, they foon fall down and die,
  And by corruption quickly taken.

Ufe then your time, ye virgins fair,
  Employ your day before 'tis evil;
Fifteen is a feafon rare,
  But five and twenty is the devil.
Juft when ripe, confent unto't,
  Hug nae mair your lanely pillow;
Women are like other fruit,
  They lofe their relifh when too mellow.

If opportunity be loſt,
  You'll find it hard to be regained;
Which now I may tell to my coſt,
  Tho' but myſell nane can be blamed:
If then your fortune you reſpect,
  Take the occaſion when it offers;
Nor a true lover's ſuit neglect,
  Leſt you be ſcoff'd for being ſcoffers.

I, by his fond expreſſions, thought,
  That in his love he'd ne'er prove changing;
But now, alas! 'tis turn'd to nought,
  And, paſt my hope, he's gane a-ranging.
Dear maidens, then take my advice,
  And let na coyneſs prove your ruin;
For if ye be o'er fooliſh nice,
  Your ſuitors will give over wooing.

Then *maidens auld* you nam'd will be,
  And in that fretfu' rank be number'd,
As lang as life; and when ye die,
  With leading apes be ever cumber'd:
A puniſhment, and hated brand,
  With which nane of us are contented;
Then be not wife behind the hand,
  That the miſtake may be prevented.

✢:✦:✦:✦:✦:✦:✦:✦:✦:✦:✦:✦

The young Ladies' Thanks to the repenting Virgin, for her ſeaſonable Advice.

O VIRGIN kind! we canna tell
    How many many thanks we owe you,
For pointing out to us ſae well
    Thoſe very rocks that did o'erthrow you;

And we your leſſon ſae ſhall mind,
  That e'en tho' a' our kin had ſwore it,
Ere we ſhall be an hour behind,
  We'll take a year or twa before it.

We'll catch all winds blaw in our ſails,
  And ſtill keep out our flag and pinnet;
If young Philander anes aſſails
  To ſtorm love's fort, then he ſhall win it:
We may indeed, for modeſty,
  Preſent our forces for reſiſtance;
But we ſhall quickly lay them by,
  And contribute to his aſſiſtance.

The Stepdaughter's Relief.

Tune—*The kirk wad let me be.*

I WAS anes a well tocher'd laſs,
  My mither left dollars to me;
But now I'm brought to a poor paſs,
  My ſtepdame has gart them flee.
My father he's aften frae hame,
  And ſhe plays the deel with his gear;
She neither has lawtith nor ſhame,
  And keeps the hale houſe in a ſteer.

She's barmy-fac'd, thriftleſs, and bauld,
  And gars me aft fret and repine;
While hungry, ha'f naked, and cauld,
  I ſee her deſtroy what's mine:
But ſoon I might hope a revenge,
  And ſoon of my ſorrows be free,
My poortith to plenty wad change,
  If ſhe were hung up on a tree.

Quoth Ringan, wha lang time had loo'd
  This bonny lafs tenderly,
I'll take thee, fweet May, in thy fnood,
  Gif thou wilt gae hame with me.
'Tis only yourfell that I want,
  Your kindnefs is better to me
Than a' that your ftepmother, fcant
  Of grace, now has taken frae thee.

I'm but a young farmer, 'tis true,
  And ye are the fprout of a laird;
But I have milk-cattle enow,
  And rowth of good rucks in my yard;
Ye fhall have naething to fafh ye,
  Sax fervants fhall jouk to thee:
Then kilt up thy coats, my laffie,
  And gae thy ways hame with me.

The maiden her reafon employ'd,
  Not thinking the offer amifs,
Confented;—while Ringan o'erjoy'd,
  Receiv'd her with mony a kifs.
And now fhe fits blythly fingan,
  And joking her drunken ftepdame,
Delighted with her dear Ringan,
  That makes her goodwife at hame.

✥✥✥

Jeany, where has thou been?

O JEANY, Jeany, where has thou been?
  Father and mother are feeking of thee;
Ye have been ranting, playing the wanton,
  Keeping of Jocky company.
O Betty, *I've been to hear the mill clack,*
  Getting meal ground for the family;
As fow as it gade I brang hame the fack,
  For the miller has taken nae mowter frae me.

Ha! Jeany, Jeany, there's meal on your back,
  The miller's a wanton billy, and flee;
Tho' victual's come hame again hale, what-reck,
  I fear he has taken his mowter aff thee.
And, Betty, ye spread your linen to bleach,
  When that was done, where cou'd you be?
Ha! lass, I saw ye slip down the hedge,
  And wanton Willy was following thee.

Ay, Jeany, Jeany, ye gaed to the kirk;
  But when it skail'd, where cou'd thou be?
Ye came na hame till it was mirk,
  They say the kissing clerk came wi' ye.
O silly lassie, what wilt thou do?
  If thou grow great, they'll heez thee hie.
Look to yoursell, if Jock prove true:
  The clerk frae creepies will keep me free. Q.

SONG.

Tune—Last time I came o'er the moor.

YE blythest lads and lasses gay,
  Hear what my sang disclofes.
As I ae morning sleeping lay
  Upon a bank of roses,
Young Jamie whisking o'er the mead,
  By good luck chanc'd to spy me;
He took his bonnet aff his head,
  And saftly sat down by me.

Jamie tho' I right meikle priz'd,
  Yet now I wadna ken him;
But with a frown my face disguis'd,
  And strave away to send him:

But fondly he ſtill nearer preſt,
　And by my ſide down lying,
His beating heart thumped ſae faſt,
　I thought the lad was dying.

But ſtill refolving to deny,
　And angry paſſion feigning,
I aften roughly ſhot him by,
　With words full of difdaining.
Poor Jamie bawk'd, nae favour wins,
　Went aff much difcontented;
But I in truth, for a' my ſins,
　Ne'er haff ſae fair repented.　　X.

The Cock Laird.

A Cock laird fou cadgie,
　With Jenny did meet,
He haws'd her, he kifs'd her,
　And ca'd her his fweet.
Wilt thou gae alang
　Wi' me, Jenny, Jenny?
Thoufe be my ain lemman,
　Jo Jenny, quoth he.

If I gae alang wi' ye,
　Ye maunna fail
To feaſt me with caddels
　And good hacket-kail.
The deel's in your nicety,
　Jenny, quoth he,
Mayna bannocks of bear-meal
　Be as good for thee?

And I maun hae pinners,
　With pearling fet round,
A ſkirt of puddy,
　And a waſtecoat of brown.

Awa with fic vanities,
　　Jenny, quoth he,
For kurchis and kirtles
　　Are fitter for thee.

My lairdſhip can yield me
　　As meikle a-year,
As had us in pottage
　　And good knockit bear:
But having nae tenants,
　　O Jenny, Jenny,
To buy ought I ne'er have
　　A penny, quoth he.

The borrowſtoun merchants
　　Will ſell ye on tick,
For we maun hae braw things,
　　Albeit they ſoud break.
When broken, frae care
　　The fools are ſet free,
When we make them lairds
　　In the Abbey, quoth ſhe.

The Soger Laddie.

MY ſoger laddie is over the ſea,
　　And he will bring gold and money to me;
And when he comes hame, he'll make me a lady;
My bleſſing gang with my ſoger laddie.

My doughty laddie is handſome and brave,
And can as a ſoger and lover behave;
True to his country, to love he is ſteady,
There's few to compare with my ſoger laddie.

Shield him, ye angels, frae death in alarms,
Return him with laurels to my langing arms;

Syne frae all my care he'll pleasantly free me,
When back to my wishes my foger ye gie me.

O soon may his honours bloom fair on his brow,
As quickly they must, if he get his due :
For in noble actions his courage is ready,
Which makes me delight in my foger laddie.

The Archers' March.

SOUND, sound the music, sound it,
    Let hills and dales rebound it,
Let hills and dales rebound it,
      In praise of archery :
Its origin divine is,
The practice brave and fine is,
Which generously inclines us
      To guard our liberty.

    Art by the gods employed,
By which heroes enjoyed,
By which heroes enjoyed
      The wreaths of victory.
The deity of Parnassus,
The god of soft caresses,
Chaste Cynthia and her lasses,
      Delight in archery.

    See, see yon bow extended !
'Tis Jove himself that bends it,
'Tis Jove himself that bends it,
      O'er clouds on high it glows.
All nations, Turks and Parthians,
The Tartars and the Scythians,
The Arabs, Moors, and Indians,
      With bravery draw their bows.

Our own true records tell us,
That none cou'd e'er excel us,
That none cou'd e'er excel us
  In martial archery :
With fhafts our fires engaging,
Oppos'd the Romans raging,
Defeat the fierce Norvegian,
  And fpared few Danes to flee.

Witnefs Largs and Loncartie,
Dunkel and Aberlemny,
Dunkel and Aberlemny,
  Roflin and Bannockburn,
The Cheviots——all the border,
Were bowmen in brave order,
Told enemies, if furder
  They mov'd, they'd ne'er return.

Sound, found the mufic, found it,
Let hills and dales rebound it,
Let hills and dales rebound it,
  In praife of archery :
Us'd as a game it pleafes,
The mind to joy it raifes,
And throws off all difeafes
  Of lazy luxury.

Now, now our care beguiling,
When all the year looks fmiling,
When all the year looks fmiling,
  With healthful harmony :
The fun in glory glowing,
With morning-dew beftowing,
Sweet fragrance, life, and growing,
  To flowers and every tree.

'Tis now the archers royal,
An hearty band and loyal,
An hearty band and loyal,
  That in juft thoughts agree :

Appear in ancient bravery,
Defpifing all bafe knavery,
Which tends to bring in flavery
    Souls worthy to live free.

Sound, found the mufic, found it,
Fill up the glafs and round wi't,
Fill up the glafs and round wi't,
    Health and profperity
T' our great CHIEF and *Officers*,
T' our *Prefident* and *Counfellors:*
To all, who, like their brave forbears,
    Delight in archery.

Largs, where the Norwegians, headed by their valiant King HACO, were, *anno* 1263, totally defeated by ALEXANDER III. King of Scots; the heroic ALEXANDER, Great Steward of Scotland, commanded the right wing.

Loncartie, near Perth, where King KENNETH III. obtained the victory over the Danes, which was principally owing to the valour and refolution of the firft brave HAY, and his two fons.

Dunkel, here, and in Kyle, and on the banks of Tay, our great King CORBREDUS GALDUS, in three battles, overthrew 30,000 Romans, in the reign of the Emperor DOMITIAN.

Aberlemny, four miles from Brechin, where King MALCOLM II. obtained a glorious victory over the united armies of Danes, Norwegians, and Cumbrians, etc., commanded by SUENO, King of Denmark, and his warlike fon Prince CANUTE.

Roflin, about five miles fouth of Edinburgh, where 10,000 Scots, led by Sir JOHN CUMIN and Sir SIMON FRASER, defeated in three battles, in one day, 30,000 of their enemies, *anno* 1303.

The battles of Bannockburn and Cheviot, etc., are fo well known, that they require no notes.

OF CHOICE SONGS.

The following SONGS *sung in their proper places, at acting of the* GENTLE SHEPHERD.

SANG I.

The wawking of the faulds.

Sung by PATIE.

MY Peggy is a young thing,
　　Juſt enter'd in her teens,
Fair as the day, and ſweet as May,
Fair as the day, and always gay.
　　My Peggy is a young thing,
　　　And I'm not very auld,
　　Yet well I like to meet her at
　　　The wawking of the fauld.

My Peggy ſpeaks ſae ſweetly,
　　Whene'er we meet alane,
I wiſh nae mair, to lay my care.
I wiſh nae mair of a' that's rare.
　　My Peggy ſpeaks ſae ſweetly,
　　　To a' the lave I'm cauld;
　　But ſhe gars a' my ſpirits glow
　　　At wawking of the fauld.

My Peggy ſmiles ſae kindly,
　　Whene'er I whiſper love,
That I look down on a' the town,
That I look down upon a crown.
　　My Peggy ſmiles ſae kindly,
　　　It makes me blyth and bauld,
　　And naething gi'es me ſic delight,
　　　As wawking of the fauld.

My Peggy ſings ſae ſaftly,
　　When on my pipe I play;
By a' the reſt it is confeſs'd,
By a' the reſt, that ſhe ſings beſt.

My Peggy sings sae saftly,
    And in her sangs are tald,
With innocence, the wale of sense,
    At wawking of the fauld.

Sang II.

Fy gar rub her o'er with strae.

Sung by Patie.

DEAR Roger, if your Jenny geck,
    And answer kindness with a slight,
Seem unconcern'd at her neglect,
    For women in a man delight:
But them despise who're soon defeat,
    And with a simple face give way
To a repulse;—then be not blate,
    Push bauldly on, and win the day.

When maidens, innocently young,
    Say aften what they never mean,
Ne'er mind their pretty lying tongue,
    But tent the language of their een.
If these agree, and she persist
    To answer all your love with hate,
Seek elsewhere to be better bless'd,
    And let her sigh when 'tis too late.

Sang III.

Polwart on the green.

Sung by Peggy.

THE dorty will repent,
    If lover's heart grow cauld,
And nane her smiles will tent,
    Soon as her face looks auld.

The dawted bairn thus takes the pet,
    Nor eats, tho' hunger crave,
Whimpers and tarrows at its meat,
    And's laugh'd at by the lave;
They jeft it till the dinner's paft:
    Thus, by itfell abus'd,
The fool thing is oblig'd to faft,
    Or eat what they've refus'd.

Sang IV.

O dear mother, what fhall I do?

Sung by JENNY.

O DEAR Peggy, love's beguiling,
    We ought not to truft his fmiling;
Better far to do as I do,
    Left a harder luck betide you.
Laffes, when their fancy's carry'd,
    Think of nought but to be marry'd;
Running to a life deftroys
    Heartfome, free, and youthfu' joys.

Sang V.

How can I be fad on my wedding day?

Sung by PEGGY.

HOW fhall I be fad when a hufband I hae,
    That has better fenfe than any of thae
Sour weak filly fellows, that ftudy like fools
To fink their ain joy, and make their wives fnools?
The man who is prudent, ne'er lightlies his wife,
Or with dull reproaches encourages ftrife;
He praifes her virtues, and ne'er will abufe
Her for a fmall failing, but find an excufe.

Sang VI.

Nancy's to the greenwood gane.

Sung by Jenny.

I YIELD, dear laffie, ye have won,
   And there is nae denying,
That fure as light flows frae the fun,
   Frae love proceeds complying;
For a' that we can do or fay
   'Gainft love, nae thinker heeds us;
They ken our bofoms lodge the fae
   That by the heart-ftrings leads us.

Sang VII.

Cauld kail in Aberdeen.

Sung by Glaud or Symon.

CAULD be the rebels caft,
   Oppreffors bafe and bloody,
I hope we'll fee them at the laft
   Strung a' up in a woody.
Bleft be he of worth and fenfe,
   And ever high his ftation,
That bravely ftands in the defence
   Of confcience, king, and nation.

Sang VIII.

Mucking of Geordy's byre.

Sung by Symon.

THE laird who in riches and honour
   Wad thrive, fhould be kindly and free,
Nor rack the poor tenants, who labour
   To rife aboon poverty:

Elfe, like the pack-horfe that's unfother'd,
   And burden'd, will tumble down faint;
Thus virtue by hardſhip is ſmother'd,
   And rackers aft tine their rent.

Sang IX.

Carle and the King come.

Sung by Mause.

PEGGY, now the king's come,
   Peggy, now the King's come,
Thou may dance, and I ſhall ſing,
   Peggy, ſince the king's come.
Nae mair the hawkies thou ſhalt milk,
But change thy plaiding coat for ſilk,
And be a lady of that ilk,
   Now, Peggy, ſince the king's come.

Sang X.

Winter was cauld, and my claithing was thin.

Sung by Peggy and Patie.

Peggy.

WHEN firſt my dear laddie gade to the green hill,
   And I at ew-milking firſt fey'd my young ſkill,
To bear the milk-bowie, nae pain was to me.
When I at the bughting forgather'd with thee.

Patie.

When corn-riggs wav'd yellow, and blew hether bells
Bloom'd bonny on moorland and ſweet riſing fells,
Nae birns, brier, or breckens gave trouble to me,
If I found the berries right ripen'd for thee.

PEGGY.

When thou ran, or wreftled, or putted the ftane,
And came aff the victor, my heart was ay fain :
Thy ilka fport manly gave pleafure to me,
For nane can put, wreftle, or run fwift as thee.

PATIE.

Our Jenny fings faftly the *Cowden broom-knows*,
And Rofie lilts fweetly the *Milking the ews;*
There's few *Jenny Nettles* like Nancy can fing,
At *Throw the wood laddie*, Befs gars our lugs ring :
But when my dear Peggy fings with better fkill,
The *Boat-man, Tweed-fide*, or the *Lafs of the mill*,
'Tis many times fweeter and pleafing to me :
For tho' they fing nicely, they cannot like thee.

PEGGY.

How eafy can laffes trow what they defire?
And praifes fae kindly increafes love's fire :
Give me ftill this pleafure, my ftudy fhall be
To make myfelf better and fweeter for thee.

SANG XI.

By the delicious warmnefs of thy mouth.

Sung by PATIE and PEGGY.

Printed in the PASTORAL, *and in this* MISCELLANY,
Vol I., p. 77.

SANG XII.

Happy Clown.

Sung by Sir WILLIAM.

HID from himfelf, now by the dawn
He ftarts as frefh as rofes blawn,

And ranges o'er the heights and lawn,
    After his bleating flocks:
Healthful, and innocently gay
He chants, and whiftles out the day;
Untaught to fmile and then betray,
    Like courtly weather-cocks.

  Life happy from ambition free,
Envy and vile hypocrifie,
Where truth and love with joys agree,
    Unfully'd with a crime:
Unmov'd with what difturbs the great,
In propping of their pride and ftate,
He lives, and, unafraid of fate,
    Contented fpends his time.

Sang XIII.

Leith-Wynd.

Sung by Jenny and Roger.

WERE I affur'd you'll conftant prove,
    You fhould nae mair complain,
The eafy maid, befet with love,
    Few words will quickly gain;
For I muft own, now fince you're free,
    This too fond heart of mine
Has lang, a black-fole true to thee,
    Wifh'd to be pair'd with thine.

Roger.

I'm happy now, ah! let my head
    Upon thy breaft recline;
The pleafure ftrikes me nearhand dead!
    Is Jenny then fae kind!——

O let me brifs thee to my heart!
   And round my arms entwine:
Delytful thought! we'll never part:
   Come prefs thy mouth to mine.

Sang XIV.

O'er Bogie.

Sung by Jenny.

WELL, I agree, you're fure of me;
   Next to my father gae,
Make him content to give confent,
   He'll hardly fay you nay:
For you have what he wad be at,
   And will commend you weel,
Since parents auld think love grows cauld,
   Where bairns want milk and meal.

Shou'd he deny, I carena by,
   He'd contradict in vain.
Tho' a' my kin had faid and fworn,
   But thee I will have nane.
Then never range, or learn to change,
   Like thofe in high degree:
And if you prove faithful in love,
   You'll find nae fault in me.

Sang XV.

Wat ye wha I met yeftreen.

Sung by Sir William.

NOW from rufticity, and love,
   Whofe flames but over lowly burn,
My gentle fhepherd muft be drove,
   His foul muft take another turn:

      As the rough diamond from the mine,
        In breaking only shews its light,
      Till polishing has made it shine;
        Thus learning makes the genius bright.

Sang XVI.

Kirk wad let me be.

Sung by Patie.

DUTY and part of reason
    Plead strong on the parent's side,
Which love superior calls treason;
    The strongest must be obey'd:
For now, tho' I'm one of the gentry,
    My constancy falshood repels;
For change on my heart has no entry,
    Still there my dear Peggy excels.

Sang XVII.

Woes my heart that we should sunder.

Sung by Peggy.

SPEAK on,—speak thus, and still my grief,
    Hold up a heart that's sinking under
These fears, that soon will want relief,
    When Pate must from his Peggy sunder.
A gentler face, and silk attire,
    A lady rich in beauty's blossom,
Alake poor me! will now conspire
    To steal thee from thy Peggy's bosom.

No more the shepherd who excell'd
  The rest, whose wit made them to wonder,
Shall now his Peggy's praises tell;
  Ah! I can die, but never funder.
Ye meadows where we often stray'd,
  Ye banks where we were wont to wander,
Sweet-scented rucks, round which we play'd,
  You'll lose your sweets when we're asunder.

Again, ah! shall I never creep
  Around the know with silent duty,
Kindly to watch thee while asleep,
  And wonder at thy manly beauty?
Hear, heaven, while solemnly I vow,
  Tho' thou shouldst prove a wand'ring lover,
Through life to thee I shall prove true,
  Nor be a wife to any other.

Sang XVIII.

Tweed-side.

Sung by Peggy.

WHEN hope was quite sunk in despair,
  My heart it was going to break;
My life appear'd worthless my care,
  But now I will sav't for thy sake.
Where-e'er my love travels by day,
  Where-ever he lodges by night,
With me his dear image shall stay,
  And my soul keep him ever in sight.

With patience I'll wait the long year,
  And study the gentlest charms;
Hope time away till thou appear,
  To lock thee for ay in those arms.

Whilſt thou waſt a ſhepherd, I priz'd
   No higher degree in this life;
But now I'll endeavour to riſe
   To a height that's becoming thy wife.

For beauty that's only ſkin-deep,
   Muſt fade like the gowans in May;
But inwardly rooted, will keep
   For ever, without a decay.
Nor age, nor the changes of life,
   Can quench the fair fire of love,
If virtue's ingrain'd in the wife,
   And the huſband have ſenſe to approve.

Sang XIX.

Buſh aboon Traquair.

Sung by Peggy.

AT ſetting day and riſing morn,
   With ſoul that ſtill ſhall love thee,
I'll aſk of heav'n thy ſafe return,
   With all that can improve thee.
I'll viſit oft the birken buſh,
   Where firſt thou kindly told me
Sweet tales of love, and hid my bluſh,
   Whilſt round thou didſt infold me.

To all our haunts I will repair,
   By greenwood, ſhaw, or fountain;
Or where the ſummer-day I'd ſhare
   With thee, upon yon mountain.
There will I tell the trees and flow'rs,
   From thoughts unfeign'd and tender,
By vows you're mine, by love is yours
   A heart which cannot wander.

Sang XX.

Bonny grey-ey'd morn.

Sung by Sir William.

THE bonny grey-ey'd morning begins to peep,
    And darkness flies before the rising ray,
The hearty hynd starts from his lazy sleep,
    To follow healthful labours of the day;
Without a guilty sting to wrinkle his brow,
    The lark and the linnet 'tend his levee,
And he joins their concert, driving his plow,
    From toil of grimace and pageantry free.

While fluster'd with wine, or madden'd with loss
    Of half an estate, the prey of a main,
The drunkard and gamester tumble and toss,
    Wishing for calmness and slumber in vain.
Be my portion health and quietness of mind,
    Plac'd at due distance from parties and state,
Where neither ambition, nor avarice blind,
    Reach him who has happiness link'd to his fate.

On our Ladies being dressed in Scots manufactory, at a public Assembly.

SONG.

Tune—O'er the hills and far away.

LET meaner beauties use their art,
    And range both Indies for their dress,
Our fair can captivate the heart
    In native weeds, nor look the less.

More bright unborrow'd beauties ſhine,
    The artleſs ſweetneſs of each face
Sparkles with luſtres more divine,
    When freed of every foreign grace.

The tawny nymph on ſcorching plains,
    May uſe the aid of gems and paint,
Deck with brocade and Tyrian ſtains
    Features of ruder form and taint.
What Caledonian ladies wear,
    Or from the lint or woollen twine,
Adorn'd by all their ſweets, appear
    Whate'er we can imagine fine.

Apparel neat becomes the fair,
    The dirty dreſs may lovers cool;
But clean, our maids need have no care,
    If clad in linen, ſilk or wool.
T' adore Myrtilla who can ceaſe?
    Her *active charms* our praiſe demand,
Clad in a mantua, from the fleece,
    Spun by her own delighted hand.

Who can behold Califta's eyes,
    Her breaſt, her cheek, and ſnowy arms,
And mind what artiſts can deviſe,
    To rival more ſuperior charms?
Compar'd with thoſe, the diamond's dull,
    Lawns, ſatins, and the velvets fade;
The foul with her attractions full,
    Can never be by theſe betray'd.

Sapphira, all o'er native ſweets,
    Not the falſe glare of dreſs regards,
Her wit, her character completes,
    Her ſmile her lovers ſighs rewards.

When such first beauties lead the way,
   Th' inferior rank will follow soon;
Then arts no longer shall decay,
   But trade encourag'd be in tune.

Millions of fleeces shall be wove,
   And flax that on the valleys blooms,
Shall make the naked nations love
   And bless the labours of our looms:
We have enough, nor want from them,
   But trifles hardly worth our care,
Yet for these trifles let them claim
   What food and cloth we have to spare.

How happy's Scotland in her fair!
   Her amiable daughters shall,
By acting thus with virtuous care,
   Again the golden age recall:
Enjoying them, Edina ne'er
   Shall miss a court; but soon advance
In wealth, when thus the lov'd appear
   Around the scenes, or in the dance.

Barbarity shall yield to sense,
   And lazy pride to useful arts,
When such dear angels in defence
   Of virtue thus engage their hearts.
Bless'd guardians of our joys and wealth,
   True fountains of delight and love,
Long bloom your charms, fix'd be your health,
   Till tir'd with earth ye mount above.

Hardyknute.

A fragment of an old heroic ballad.

I.

STATELY ſtept he eaſt the wa,
  And ſtately ſtept he weſt,
Full ſeventy years he now had ſeen,
  With ſcarce ſeven years of reſt.
He liv'd when Britons breach of faith
  Wrought Scotland meikle wae:
And ay his ſword tauld to their coſt,
  He was their deadly fae.

II.

Hie on a hill his caſtle ſtude,
  With halls and towers a hight,
And guidly chambers fair to ſee,
  Where he lodg'd mony a knight.
His dame ſae pierleſs anes and fair,
  For chaſte and beauty deimt,
Nae marrow had in all the land,
  Save Elenor the Queen.

III.

Full thirteen ſons to him ſhe bare,
  All men of valour ſtout:
In bluidy fight, with ſword in hand,
  Nyne loſt their lives bot doubt;
Four yet remain, lang may they live
  To ſtand by liege and land:
Hie was their fame, hie was their might,
  And hie was their command.

IV.

Great love they bare to Fairly fair,
    Their fifter faft and deir,
Her girdle fhawd her middle jimp,
    And gowden glift her hair.
What waefou wae her bewtie bred?
    Waefou to young and auld,
Waefou I trou to kyth and kin,
    As ftory ever tauld.

V.

The king of Norfe in fummer-tide,
    Puft up with power and might,
Landed in fair Scotland the ifle,
    With mony a hardy knight:
The tidings to our gude Scots King
    Came as he fat at dyne,
With noble chiefs in brave array,
    Drinking the blude-red wyne.

VI.

"To horfe, to horfe, my royal liege,
    Your faes ftand on the ftrand,
Full twenty thoufand glittering fpears
    The king of Norfe commands."
Bring me my fteed, Madge, dapple gray,
    Our gude king raife and cry'd;
A truftier beaft in all the land
    A Scots king never fey'd.

VII.

Go, little page, tell Hardyknute,
    That lives on hill fo hie,
To draw his fword the dreid of faes,
    And hafte and follow me.

The little page flew fwift as dart
  Flung by his mafter's arm,
Come down, come down, Lord Hardyknute,
  And redd your king frae harm.

VIII.

Then reid, reid grew his dark-brown cheiks,
  Sae did his dark-brown brow;
His looks grew keen as they were wont
  In dangers great to do;
He has tane a horn as green as grafs,
  And gien five founds fae fhrill,
That trees in greenwood fhook thereat,
  Sae loud rang ilka hill.

IX.

His fons in manly fport and glie,
  Had paft the fummer's morn,
When lo! down in a graffy dale,
  They heard their father's horn.
That horn, quoth they, *ne'er founds in peace,*
  We have other fport to byde;
And foon they hey'd them up the hill,
  And foon were at his fyde.

X.

Late, late yeftreen I weind in peace,
  To end my lengthened life,
My age might weill excufe my arm,
  Frae manly feats of ftrife;
But now that Norfe does proudly boaft
  Fair Scotland to enthrall,
It's ne'er be faid of Hardyknute,
  He fear'd to fight or fall.

XI.

Robin of Rothsay, bend thy bow,
  Thy arrow shoot so leil,
Mony a comely countenance
  They have turn'd to deidly pale:
Brade Thomas, tak ye but your lance,
  Ye neid nae weapons mair,
Gif ye fight weil as ye did anes
  'Gainst Westmorland's fierce heir.

XII.

Malcom, light of foot as stag
  That runs in forest wyld,
Get me my thousands three of men
  Well bred to sword and shield:
Bring me my horse and harnisine,
  My blade of metal cleir.
If faes kend but the hand it bare,
  They soon had fled for fear.

XIII.

Fareweil, my dame, sae pierless good,
  And took her by the hand,
Fairer to me in age you seem,
  Than maids for beauty fam'd:
My youngest son sall here remain
  To guard these stately towirs,
And shut the silver bolt that keips
  Sae fast your painted bowirs.

XIV.

And first she wet her comely cheiks,
  And then her boddice green,
Hir silken cords of twirtle twist,
  Weil plet with silver sheen:

And apron set with mony a dyce
 Of needle-wark sae rare,
Wove by nae hand, as ye may guess,
 Save that of Fairly fair.

XV.

And he has ridden owre muir and moss,
 Owre hills and mony a glen,
When he came to a wounded knight
 Making a heavy mane;
Here maun I lye, here maun I dye,
 By treacherous false Gyles;
Witless I was that e'er gave faith
 To wicked woman's smyles.

XVI.

Sir Knight, gin ye were in my bowir,
 To lean on silken seat,
My lady's kindly care you'd prove,
 Wha neir kend deidly hate;
Hirself wald watch ye all the day,
 Her maids a deid of nicht;
And Fairly fair your heart wald cheir,
 As she stands in your sight.

XVII.

Arise, young knight, and mount your steid,
 Full lowns the shynand day,
Chuse frae my menzie whom ye please
 To lead ye on the way.
With smyless look and visage wan,
 The wounded knight reply'd,
Kind chiftain, your intent pursue,
 For heir I maun abyde.

XVIII.

To me nae after day nor night
    Can eir be sweit or fair,
But soon beneath some drapping trie,
    Cauld death fall end my care.
With him nae pleading might prevail,
    Brave Hardyknute to gain,
With fairest words and reason strang,
    Strave courteously in vain.

XIX.

Syne he has gane far hynd attowre,
    Lord Chattan's land sae wyde,
That lord a worthy wight was ay,
    When faes his courage sey'd:
Of Pictish race by mother's syde,
    When Picts rul'd Caledon,
Lord Chattan claim'd the princely maid,
    When he sav'd Pictish crown.

XX.

Now with his fierce and stalwart train,
    He reach'd a rising height,
Whair braid encampit on the dale,
    Norse army lay in sight;
Yonder, my valiant sons and seirs,
    Our raging ravers wait
On the unconquer'd Scottish swaird,
    To try with us their fate.

XXI.

Mak orisons to him that sav'd
    Our sauls upon the rude,
Syne bravely shaw your veins are fill'd
    With Caledonian blude.

Then furth he drew his trufty glaive,
  While thoufands all around,
Drawn frae their fheaths glanc'd in the fun,
  And loud the bougils found.

XXII.

To join his king adoun the hill
  In hafte his march he made,
Whyle, playand pibrochs minftralls meit,
  Afore him ftately ftrade.
Thryfe welcome valiant ftoup of weir,
  Thy nation's fhield and pryde;
Thy king nae reafon has to feir
  When thou art by his fyde.

XXIII.

When bows were bent and darts were thrawn,
  For thrang fcarce cou'd they flie,
The darts clove arrows as they met,
  The arrows dart the trie.
Lang did they rage and fight full fierce,
  With little fkaith to man,
But bluddy, bluddy was the field,
  Or that lang day was dane.

XXIV.

The king of Scots that findle bruik'd
  The war that look'd like play,
Drew his braid fword, and brake his bow,
  Sen bows feim't but delay:
Quoth noble Rothfay, *Myne I'll keip,*
  I wate its bled a fcore.
Hafte up, my merry men, cry'd the king,
  As he rade on before.

XXV.

The king of Norſe he fought to find,
　With him to menſe the fight,
But on his forehead there did light
　A ſharp unſonſie ſhaft;
As he his hand put up to find
　The wound, an arrow keen,
O waefou chance! there pinn'd his hand
　In midſt between his een.

XXVI.

Revenge, revenge, cry'd Rothſay's heir,
　Your mail-coat fall nocht byde
The ſtrength and ſharpneſs of my dart;
　Then ſent it through his ſyde:
Another arrow weil he mark'd,
　It pierc'd his neck in twa,
His hands then quat the ſilver reins,
　He laigh as eard did fa.

XXVII.

Sair bleids my liege, fair, fair he bleids.
　Again with might he drew
And geſture dreid his ſturdy bow,
　Faſt the braid arrow flew.
Wae to the knight he ettled at,
　Lament now, Quene Elgried;
Hie dames too wail your darling's fall,
　His youth and comely meid.

XXVIII.

Take aff, take aff his coſtly jupe:
　(Of gold weil was it twin'd,
Knit lyke the fowler's net, through which
　His ſteilly harneſs ſhyn'd):

Take, Norfe, that gift frae me, and bid
  Him venge the blude it beirs;
Say, if he face my bended bow,
  He fure nae weapon feirs.

XXIX.

Proud Norfe, with giant body tall,
  Braid fhoulders and arms ftrong,
Cry'd, Where is Hardyknute fae fam'd,
  And feir'd at Britain's throne?
The Britons tremble at his name,
  I foon fhall make him wail
That eir my fword was made fae fharp,
  Sae faft his coat of mail.

XXX.

That brag his ftout heart could na byde,
  It lent him youthful might:
I'm Hardyknute this day, he cry'd,
  To Scotland's king I height,
To lay thee law as horfes hufe,
  My word I mean to keip;
Syne with the firft ftrake eir he ftrake,
  He garr'd his body bleid.

XXXI.

Norfe een lyke gray gofehawks ftair'd wyld,
  He fight with fhame and fpyte;
Difgrac'd is now my far-fam'd arm
  That left thee power to ftrike:
Then gave his head a blaw fae fell,
  It made him doun to ftoup,
As law as he to ladies us'd
  In courtly gyfe to lout.

XXXII.

Full foon he rais'd his bent body,
  His bow he marvell'd fair,
Sen blaws till then on him but darr'd
  As touch of Fairly fair:
Norfe ferliet too as fair as he
  To fee his ftately look,
Sae foon as eir he ftrake a fae,
  Sae foon his lyfe he took.

XXXIII.

Whair lyke a fyre to heather fet,
  Bauld Thomas did advance,
A fturdy fae with look enrag'd
  Up towards him did prance;
He fpurr'd his fteid through thickeft rank,
  The hardy youth to quell,
Wha ftood unmov'd at his approach
  His fury to repell.

XXXIV.

That fhort brown fhaft fae meanly trimm'd
  Looks lyke poor Scotland's geir,
But dreidful feims the rufty poynt!
  And loud he leugh in jeir.
Aft Briton's blude has dimm'd its fhyne,
  This poynt cut fhort their vaunt;
Syne pierc'd the boafter's bairded cheik,
  Nae time he took to taunt.

XXXV.

Short while he in his faddle fwang,
  His ftirrip was nae ftay,
Sae feible hang his unbent knee,
  Sure taken he was fey:

Swith on the hardned clay he fell,
    Right far was heard the thud,
But Thomas look'd not as he lay
    All walt'ring in his blude.

XXXVI.

With cairles geſture, mynd unmov'd,
    On raid he north the plain,
His ſeim in thrang of fierceſt ſtryfe,
    When winner ay the ſame :
Nor yet his heart dames dipeik,
    Coud meiſe faſt love to bruik,
Till vengeful Ann return'd his ſcorn,
    Then languid grew his look.

XXXVII.

In thrawis of death, with wailowit cheik,
    All panting on the plain,
The fainting corpſe of warriors lay,
    Neir to aryſe again ;
Neir to return to native land,
    Nae mair with blythſome ſounds,
To boaſt the glories of the day,
    And ſhaw their ſhyning wounds.

XXXVIII.

On Norway's coaſt the widow'd dame
    May waſh the rocks with teirs,
May lang look owre the ſhiples ſeis,
    Before hir mate appeirs.
Ceiſe, Emma, ceiſe to hope in vain,
    Thy lord lyis in the clay,
The valiant Scots nae *revers* thole
    To carry life away.

XXXIX.

There on a lie whair ftands a crofs,
　　Set up for monument,
Thoufands full fierce that fummer's day
　　Fill'd keen waris black intent.
Let Scots, while Scots, praife Hardyknute;
　　Let Norfe the name ay dreid;
Ay how he faught, aft how he fpaird,
　　Sal lateft ages reid.

XL.

Loud and chill blew weftlin wind,
　　Sair beat the heavy fhowir,
Mirk grew the night eir Hardyknute
　　Wan neir his ftately tower;
His tower that us'd with torches bleife,
　　To fhine fae far at night,
Seim'd now as black as mourning weid,
　　Nae mervel fair he feight.

XLI.

There's nae light in my lady's bowir,
　　There's nae light in my hall;
Nae blynk fhynes round my Fairly fair,
　　Nor Warp ftands on my wall.
What bodes it? Robert, Thomas fay.
　　Nae anfwer fits their dreid.
Stand back, my fons, I'll be your gyde,
　　But by they paft with fpeid.

XLII.

As faft as I haef fped owre Scotland's facs,
　　Their ceift his brag of weir,
Seir fham'd to mynd ought but his dame,
　　And maiden Fairly fair,

Black fear he felt, but what to fear,
  He wift not yet with dreid;
Sair fhook his body, fair his limbs,
  And all the warrior fled.

*   *   *   *   *   *

The Braes of Yarrow.

BUSK ye, bufk ye, my bonny bonny bride,
  Bufk ye, bufk ye, my winfome marrow,
Bufk ye, bufk ye, my bonny bonny bride,
  And let us leave the braes of Yarrow.

Where got ye that bonny bonny bride,
  Where got ye that winfome marrow?
I got her where I durft not well be feen,
  Puing the birks on the braes of Yarrow.

Weep not, weep not, my bonny bonny bride,
  Weep not, weep not, my winfome marrow,
Nor let thy heart lament to leave
  Puing the birks on the braes of Yarrow.

Why does fhe weep, thy bonny bonny bride?
  Why does fhe weep, thy winfome marrow?
And why dare ye nae mair well be feen
  Puing the birks on the braes of Yarrow?

Lang muft fhe weep, lang muft fhe, muft fhe weep,
  Lang muft fhe weep with dole and forrow,
And lang muft I nae mair well be feen,
  Puing the birks on the braes of Yarrow.

For she has tint her lover, lover dear,
    Her lover dear, the cause of sorrow;
And I have slain the comeliest swain
    That ever pu'd birks on the braes of Yarrow.

Why runs thy stream, O Yarrow, Yarrow, reid?
    Why on thy braes heard the voice of sorrow,
And why yon melancholious weeds,
    Hung on the bonny birks of Yarrow?

What's yonder floats on the rueful, rueful flood?
    What's yonder floats? O dole and sorrow!
O 'tis the comely swain I slew
    Upon the doleful braes of Yarrow.

Wash, O wash his wounds, his wounds in tears,
    His wounds in tears of dole and sorrow,
And wrap his limbs in mourning weeds,
    And lay him on the braes of Yarrow.

Then build, then build, ye sisters, sisters sad,
    Ye sisters sad, his tomb with sorrow,
And weep around in woful wise,
    His helpless fate on the braes of Yarrow.

Curse ye, curse ye his useless, useless shield,
    My arm that wrought the deed of sorrow,
The fatal spear that pierc'd his breast,
    His comely breast on the braes of Yarrow.

Did I not warn thee not to, not to love,
    And warn from fight, but to my sorrow,
Too rashly bold, a stronger arm
    Thou mett'st, and fell on the braes of Yarrow.

Sweet fmells the birk, green grows, green grows the
    Yellow on Yarrow's braes the gowan,   [grafs,
Fair hangs the apple frae the rock,
    Sweet the wave of Yarrow flowan.

Flows Yarrow fweet, as fweet, as fweet flows Tweed,
    As green its grafs, its gowan as yellow,
As fweet fmells on its braes the birk,
    The apple from its rocks as mellow.

Fair was thy love, fair, fair indeed thy love,
    In flow'ry bands thou didft him fetter;
Tho' he was fair, and well belov'd again,
    Than me he never lov'd thee better.

Bufk ye, then bufk, my bonny bonny bride,
    Bufk ye, then bufk, my winfome marrow,
Bufk ye, and loe me on the banks of Tweed,
    And think nae mair on the braes of Yarrow.

How can I bufk a bonny bonny bride,
    How can I bufk a winfome marrow,
How loe him on the banks of Tweed,
    That flew my love on the braes of Yarrow?

O Yarrow fields, may never, never rain,
    No dew thy tender bloffoms cover,
For there was vilely kill'd my love,
    My love as he had not been a lover.

The boy put on his robes, his robes of green,
    His purple veft, 'twas my awn fewing,
Ah! wretched me, I little, little knew,
    He was in thefe to meet his ruin.

The boy took out his milk-white, milk-white steed,
  Unheedful of my dole and sorrow,
But ere the toofal of the night,
  He lay a corpse on the braes of Yarrow.

Much I rejoic'd that woful, woful day,
  I sung, my voice the woods returning;
But lang ere night the spear was flown
  That slew my love, and left me mourning.

What can my barbarous, barbarous father do,
  But with his cruel rage pursue me?
My lover's blood is on thy spear;
  How canst thou, barbarous man, then woo me?

My happy sisters may be, may be proud,
  With cruel and ungentle scoffing,
May bid me seek on Yarrow's braes
  My lover nail'd in his coffin.

My brother Douglas may upbraid,
  And strive with threat'ning words to move me;
My lover's blood is on thy spear;
  How canst thou ever bid me love thee?

Yes, yes, prepare the bed, the bed of love,
  With bridal sheets my body cover,
Unbar, ye bridal maids, the door,
  Let in the expected husband lover.

But who the expected husband, husband is?
  His hands, methinks, are bath'd in slaughter.
Ah me! what ghastly spectre's yon,
  Comes, in his pale shroud, bleeding after?

Pale as he is, here lay him, lay him down,
　　O lay his cold head on my pillow;
Take aff, take aff thefe bridal weeds,
　　And crown my careful head with yellow.

Pale tho' thou art, yet beft, yet beft belov'd,
　　O could my warmth to life reftore thee;
Yet ly all night between my breafts,
　　No youth lay ever there before thee.

Pale, pale indeed, O lovely, lovely youth!
　　Forgive, forgive fo foul a flaughter,
And ly all night between my breafts,
　　No youth fhall ever ly thereafter.

Return, return, O mournful, mournful bride,
　　Return and dry thy ufelefs forrow,
Thy lover heeds nought of thy fighs,
　　He lies a corpfe on the braes of Yarrow.

The end of the SECOND VOLUME.

www.ingramcontent.com/pod-product-compliance
Lightning Source LLC
Chambersburg PA
CBHW031351230426
43670CB00006B/509